THE
DECADENT
VEGETABLE
COOKBOOK

THE DECADENT VEGETABLE COOKBOOK

13-Digit ISBN: 978-1-60433-969-7
10-Digit ISBN: 1-60433-969-1

This book may be ordered by mail from the publisher. Please include $5.99 for postage and handling. Please support your local bookseller first!

Books published by Cider Mill Press Book Publishers are available at special discounts for bulk purchases in the United States by corporations, institutions, and other organizations. For more information, please contact the publisher.

Cider Mill Press Book Publishers
"Where good books are ready for press"
PO Box 454
12 Spring Street
Kennebunkport, Maine 04046
Visit us online!
www.cidermillpress.com

Typography: Black Jack, Garamond, Gotham

Image Credits: Photos on pages 13, 14, 38, 64, 78, 85, 89, 90, 93, 94, 97, 102, 119, 120, 124, 127, 128, 131, 132, 135, 136, 140, 143, 144, 151, 152, 155, 156, 159, 160, 164, 170, 186, 189, 206, 237, 241, 242, 245, 246, 250, 253, 278, 293, 302, 305, 306, 314, and 317 courtesy of Cider Mill Press Book Publishers.
All other photos used under official license from Shutterstock.

Printed in China

1 2 3 4 5 6 7 8 9 0

First Edition

THE DECADENT VEGETABLE COOKBOOK

Over 150 Satisfying Meatless Recipes

CIDER MILL PRESS

BOOK
PUBLISHERS
KENNEBUNKPORT, MAINE

TABLE *of* CONTENTS

❋ ❋ ❋

INTRODUCTION

✳ ✳ ✳

Though vegetarianism has come a long way, there remain many who feel as though they would be giving up if they decided to cut meat completely out of their diet. They worry that the rich meals that linger in the memory and the wonderful feeling of leaning back from a table feeling fully satiated will be lost. They see nothing but a boring string of salads queueing up to meet them. And so they remain blind to the wondrous flavors and innovative preparations that Mother Nature and the contemporary culinary revolution have lain at our feet.

This book intends to open everyone's eyes to the possibilities of a vegetarian diet—those that have already taken the plunge and those who are on the fence, allowing them to see that decadence and elegance are not part of what is restricted when one swears off meat. By scanning the globe for a collection of dishes that attain a level of excellence, and highlighting vegetables and varietals that are often overlooked, each trip to the supermarket's produce section or the local farmers market will suddenly carry the excitement a child feels when set loose in a candy store. Once you wrap your head around the recipes and techniques contained within, your mind will swim at the possibilities that are available for shockingly little cost, considering the enjoyment and nourishment they provide.

Everyone knows that the decision to be a vegetarian is a positive one in terms of their health. The time has come to show that the taste buds are also a beneficiary.

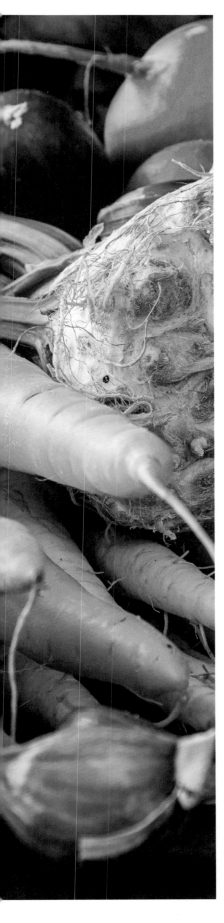

CHAPTER 1

STOCKS, SAUCES & STAPLES

A large part of taking your cooking to the next level is learning how to make helpful components such as stocks and sauces yourself, ensuring that they are always of the highest quality, and place you a couple of steps ahead when it comes time to prepare a meal.

From the rich base a homemade Vegetable Stock (see page 12) can lend your dishes to effortless and endlessly useful preparations such as Tahini Dressing (see page 20) and Romesco Sauce (see page 23), the recipes in this chapter will become the jumping off point for a number of your favorite dishes.

Vegetable Stock

YIELD: **6 CUPS**

ACTIVE TIME: **20 MINUTES**

TOTAL TIME: **3 HOURS**

A great way to make use of your vegetable trimmings. Just avoid starchy vegetables such as potatoes, as they will make the stock cloudy.

INGREDIENTS

2 TABLESPOONS OLIVE OIL

2 LARGE LEEKS, TRIMMED AND RINSED

2 LARGE CARROTS, PEELED AND SLICED

2 CELERY STALKS, SLICED

2 LARGE YELLOW ONIONS, SLICED

3 GARLIC CLOVES, UNPEELED BUT SMASHED

2 SPRIGS FRESH PARSLEY

2 SPRIGS FRESH THYME

1 BAY LEAF

8 CUPS WATER

½ TEASPOON BLACK PEPPERCORNS

SALT, TO TASTE

DIRECTIONS

1. Place the olive oil and the vegetables in a large stockpot and cook over low heat until the liquid the vegetables release has evaporated. This will allow the flavor of the vegetables to become concentrated.

2. Add the garlic, parsley, thyme, bay leaf, water, peppercorns, and salt. Raise the heat to high and bring to a boil. Reduce heat so that the stock simmers and cook for 2 hours, while skimming to remove any impurities that float to the top.

3. Strain the stock through a fine sieve, let the stock cool slightly, and place in the refrigerator, uncovered. When the stock has cooled completely, remove the fat layer and cover. The stock will keep in the refrigerator for 3 to 5 days, and in the freezer for up to 3 months.

Mushroom Stock

YIELD: **6 CUPS**

ACTIVE TIME: **15 MINUTES**

TOTAL TIME: **3 TO 4 HOURS**

Obviously, this stock can be used as the base for a soup, but it is equally effective when smaller amounts are added to a simmering dish.

INGREDIENTS

2 TABLESPOONS OLIVE OIL

3 LBS. MUSHROOMS

1 ONION, CHOPPED

1 GARLIC CLOVE, MINCED

2 BAY LEAVES

1 TABLESPOON BLACK PEPPERCORNS

2 SPRIGS THYME

1 CUP WHITE WINE

8 CUPS WATER

DIRECTIONS

1. Place the oil and mushrooms in a large stockpot and cook over low heat for 30 to 40 minutes. The longer you cook the mushrooms, the better the stock will taste, as the lengthy cook time concentrates the flavor.

2. Add the onion, garlic, bay leaves, peppercorns, and thyme and cook for 5 minutes. Add the white wine, cook 5 minutes, and then add the water.

3. Bring to a boil, reduce heat so that stock simmers, and cook for 2 to 3 hours, until you are pleased with the taste. Strain through a fine sieve, discard the solids, and refrigerate the stock until cool.

Vegetarian Dashi Broth

The base of Japan's beloved miso soup is also excellent for adding a briny element to any dish.

YIELD: **6 CUPS**

ACTIVE TIME: **10 MINUTES**

TOTAL TIME: **40 MINUTES**

INGREDIENTS

---

6 CUPS WATER

2 OZ. KOMBU

8 DRIED SHIITAKE MUSHROOMS

DIRECTIONS

---

1. Place the water and the kombu in a large saucepan and let the kombu soak for 20 minutes.

2. Remove the kombu and gently score the surface with a knife. Return the kombu to the water and bring to a boil. Remove the kombu immediately, so that the broth doesn't become bitter.

3. Add the dried shiitakes and return to a boil. Remove the saucepan from heat and let the broth stand until cool. Strain through a fine sieve, discard the solids, and refrigerate the broth until ready to use.

Blender Hollandaise

YIELD: **1 CUP**

ACTIVE TIME: **5 MINUTES**

TOTAL TIME: **5 MINUTES**

The blender puts this beloved, buttery sauce instantly within reach.

INGREDIENTS

3 LARGE EGG YOLKS

¼ TEASPOON KOSHER SALT

2 TABLESPOONS FRESH LEMON JUICE

1 STICK UNSALTED BUTTER

DIRECTIONS

1. Place the egg yolks, salt, and lemon juice in a blender and blitz until they are combined.

2. Melt the butter in a small saucepan over medium-low heat, being careful not to let it brown.

3. Turn on the blender and slowly drizzle the hot butter into the egg mixture until fully emulsified. Taste, adjust seasoning if necessary, and use immediately.

Tahini Dressing

YIELD: **2 CUPS**

ACTIVE TIME: **10 MINUTES**

TOTAL TIME: **20 MINUTES**

You can use this as the base of a creamy hummus, or to dress up a humble side of grilled vegetables.

INGREDIENTS

½ HEAD GARLIC

6 TABLESPOONS FRESH LEMON JUICE

1 TEASPOON KOSHER SALT

1 CUP TAHINI

½ TEASPOON CUMIN

ICE-COLD WATER, AS NEEDED

DIRECTIONS

1. Place the unpeeled garlic cloves and the lemon juice in the blender. Add a pinch of the salt and blitz until the mixture is a coarse puree. Let the mixture stand for 10 minutes.

2. Working over a large mixing bowl, strain the puree through a fine sieve and press down on the solids to remove as much liquid as possible. Discard the solids and add the tahini, cumin, and remaining salt to the mixing bowl. Whisk until smooth and creamy, adding water as needed if the mixture needs thinning out. Use immediately or store in the refrigerator for up to 1 week.

Romesco Sauce

YIELD: **1 CUP**

ACTIVE TIME: **5 MINUTES**

TOTAL TIME: **5 MINUTES**

This red pepper–based sauce originated in the fishing communities of Catalonia, but its bold, zippy flavor has since carried it onto tables across the globe.

INGREDIENTS

2 LARGE ROASTED RED BELL PEPPERS

1 GARLIC CLOVE, SMASHED

½ CUP SLIVERED ALMONDS, TOASTED

¼ CUP TOMATO PUREE

2 TABLESPOONS FINELY CHOPPED FLAT-LEAF PARSLEY

2 TABLESPOONS SHERRY VINEGAR

1 TEASPOON SMOKED PAPRIKA

SALT AND PEPPER, TO TASTE

½ CUP OLIVE OIL

DIRECTIONS

1. Place all of the ingredients, except for the olive oil, in a blender or food processor and pulse until the mixture is smooth.

2. Add the olive oil in a steady stream and blitz until emulsified. Season with salt and pepper and use immediately.

Basil Pesto

YIELD: **1 CUP**

ACTIVE TIME: **10 MINUTES**

TOTAL TIME: **10 MINUTES**

This simple pesto is always great to have on hand, as it will give you options in a number of preparations.

INGREDIENTS

¼ CUP WALNUTS

3 GARLIC CLOVES

SALT AND PEPPER, TO TASTE

2 CUPS FIRMLY PACKED FRESH BASIL LEAVES

½ CUP OLIVE OIL

¼ CUP GRATED PARMESAN CHEESE

¼ CUP GRATED PECORINO SARDO CHEESE

DIRECTIONS

1. Warm a small skillet over low heat for 1 minute. Add the walnuts and cook, while stirring, until they begin to give off a toasty fragrance, 2 to 3 minutes. Transfer to a plate and let cool completely.

2. Place the garlic, salt, and walnuts in a food processor or blender and pulse until the mixture is a coarse meal. Add the basil and pulse until finely minced. Transfer the mixture to a mixing bowl and add the oil in a thin stream as you quickly whisk it in.

3. Add the cheeses and stir until thoroughly incorporated. The pesto will keep in the refrigerator for up to 4 days and in the freezer for up to 3 months.

Marinara Sauce

YIELD: **8 CUPS**

ACTIVE TIME: **20 MINUTES**

TOTAL TIME: **2 HOURS**

Every great cook needs a foolproof marinara sauce, as there remains no better method to capture the flavor of fresh tomatoes.

INGREDIENTS

4 LBS. TOMATOES, QUARTERED

1 LARGE YELLOW ONION, SLICED

15 GARLIC CLOVES, CRUSHED

2 TEASPOONS FINELY CHOPPED FRESH THYME

2 TEASPOONS FINELY CHOPPED FRESH OREGANO

2 TABLESPOONS OLIVE OIL

1½ TABLESPOONS KOSHER SALT

1 TEASPOON BLACK PEPPER

2 TABLESPOONS FINELY CHOPPED FRESH BASIL

1 TABLESPOON FINELY CHOPPED FRESH PARSLEY

DIRECTIONS

1. Place all of the ingredients, except for the basil and parsley, in a Dutch oven and cook over medium heat, stirring constantly, until the tomatoes release their liquid and begin to collapse, about 10 minutes. Reduce the heat to low and cook, stirring occasionally, for about 1½ hours, or until the flavor is to your liking.

2. Stir in the basil and parsley and season to taste. The sauce will be chunky. If you prefer a smoother texture, transfer the sauce to a blender and puree before serving.

Creamy Leek Sauce

YIELD: **2 CUPS**

ACTIVE TIME: **15 MINUTES**

TOTAL TIME: **30 MINUTES**

The mild, slightly sweet-and-sour flavor of leeks makes this effortless cream sauce seem the apex of elegance.

INGREDIENTS

4 LEEKS

4 TABLESPOONS UNSALTED BUTTER

SALT, TO TASTE

1¼ CUPS HEAVY CREAM

½ CUP WHOLE MILK

½ TEASPOON WHITE PEPPER

DIRECTIONS

1. Trim away the root ends and dark green leaves of the leeks, keeping only the white and light green parts. With a sharp knife, cut each leek in half lengthwise and remove the two outer layers. Cut the halves into long, thin slivers, place them in a large bowl of water, and swish them around to remove any dirt. Drain well and pat dry.

2. Warm a large skillet over low heat for 2 to 3 minutes. Add 2 tablespoons of the butter and raise heat to medium. Once the butter has melted and stopped foaming, add the leeks and a couple pinches of salt and stir. When the leeks begin to gently sizzle, reduce heat to low, cover the pan, and cook, stirring occasionally, until the leeks become very soft and turn a slightly darker shade of green, about 20 minutes.

3. Raise heat to medium-high, add the cream, milk, and white pepper, and bring to a boil. Reduce heat to low and simmer, uncovered, until the liquid has reduced slightly, about 5 minutes. Season with salt and serve immediately.

Vegan Worcestershire Sauce

YIELD: **3 CUPS**

ACTIVE TIME: **5 MINUTES**

TOTAL TIME: **20 MINUTES**

At last, vegetarians don't have to go without the beguiling quality Worcestershire sauce adds to a dish.

INGREDIENTS

2 CUPS APPLE CIDER VINEGAR

½ CUP SOY SAUCE

¼ CUP GENTLY PACKED LIGHT BROWN SUGAR

1 TEASPOON GROUND GINGER

1 TEASPOON MUSTARD POWDER

1 TEASPOON ONION POWDER

1 GARLIC CLOVE, CRUSHED

½ TEASPOON CINNAMON

½ TEASPOON BLACK PEPPER

DIRECTIONS

1. Place all of the ingredients in a saucepan and bring to a boil over medium-high heat. Reduce heat so that the sauce simmers and cook until it has reduced by half, about 15 minutes.

2. Strain through a fine sieve, discard the solids, and let the sauce cool completely. Store in an airtight container in the refrigerator for up to 3 months.

Roasted Tomato Salsa

YIELD: **1 CUP**

ACTIVE TIME: **20 MINUTES**

TOTAL TIME: **1 HOUR AND 30 MINUTES**

Roasting the tomatoes brings out their sweet side and makes this salsa good enough to enjoy on its own.

INGREDIENTS

1 LB. RIPE TOMATOES, CORED AND HALVED

1½ TEASPOONS OLIVE OIL

SALT AND PEPPER, TO TASTE

2 TABLESPOONS MINCED YELLOW ONION

½ JALAPEÑO PEPPER, STEMMED, SEEDED, AND MINCED

1 TABLESPOON FINELY CHOPPED FRESH CILANTRO

1 TABLESPOON FRESH LIME JUICE

DIRECTIONS

1. Preheat your oven to 450°F. Place the tomatoes, olive oil, salt, and pepper in a large bowl and toss to coat. Let stand for 30 minutes.

2. Place the tomatoes, cut-side down, on a baking sheet, place them in the oven, and roast until they start to char and soften, about 10 minutes. Carefully turn the tomatoes over and cook until they start bubbling, about 5 minutes. Remove from the oven and let the tomatoes cool completely.

3. Chop the tomatoes and place them in a bowl with the remaining ingredients. Stir to combine and let stand at room temperature for 45 minutes. Taste, adjust seasoning if necessary, and serve. The salsa will keep in the refrigerator for up to 2 days.

Salsa Verde

YIELD: **1 CUP**
ACTIVE TIME: **5 MINUTES**
TOTAL TIME: **15 MINUTES**

The tart and sweet tomatillo is one of the easiest and most delicious ways to add a burst of color to your table.

INGREDIENTS

6 TOMATILLOS, HUSKED AND RINSED

8 SERRANO PEPPERS, STEMMED AND SEEDED TO TASTE

½ YELLOW ONION, CHOPPED

2 GARLIC CLOVES, MINCED

SALT, TO TASTE

¼ CUP OLIVE OIL

FRESH CILANTRO, FINELY CHOPPED, FOR GARNISH

DIRECTIONS

1. Place the tomatillos and serrano peppers in a large saucepan and cover with water. Bring to a boil and cook until the tomatillos start to lose their bright green color, about 10 minutes.

2. Drain and transfer the tomatillos and peppers to a blender. Add all of the remaining ingredients, except for the cilantro, and puree until smooth. Top with the cilantro and serve. The salsa will keep in the refrigerator for up to 2 days.

Guacamole

Wholly suitable as a side or as the centerpiece of a casual gathering.

YIELD: **2 CUPS**

ACTIVE TIME: **5 MINUTES**

TOTAL TIME: **5 MINUTES**

INGREDIENTS

2 TABLESPOONS MINCED RED ONION

ZEST AND JUICE OF 1 LIME

SALT, TO TASTE

1 JALAPEÑO PEPPER, STEMMED, SEEDED, AND MINCED

FLESH FROM 3 AVOCADOS, CHOPPED

2 TABLESPOONS CHOPPED FRESH CILANTRO

1 PLUM TOMATO, CONCASSE (SEE SIDEBAR)

DIRECTIONS

1. Place the onion, lime zest and juice, salt, and jalapeño in a mixing bowl and stir to combine.

2. Add the avocados and work the mixture with a fork until the desired consistency has been reached. Add the cilantro and tomato, stir to incorporate, and taste. Adjust seasoning if necessary and serve immediately.

TOMATO CONCASSE

Concasse, French for "to crush or grind," refers to tomatoes that have been peeled, seeded, and then chopped. To do this easily, boil enough water for a tomato to be submerged and add a pinch of salt. Prepare an ice water bath and score the top of the tomato with a paring knife. Place the tomato in the boiling water for 30 seconds, carefully remove it, and place it in the ice water bath. Once the tomato is cool, remove from the water and peel with the paring knife. Cut into quarters, remove the seeds, and chop.

Kimchi

YIELD: **4 CUPS**

ACTIVE TIME: **30 MINUTES**

TOTAL TIME: **3 TO 7 DAYS**

Simple, flavorful, and versatile, kimchi is the perfect introduction to your new best friend: fermentation.

INGREDIENTS

1 HEAD NAPA CABBAGE, CUT INTO STRIPS

½ CUP KOSHER SALT

2 TABLESPOONS MINCED GINGER

3 GARLIC CLOVES, MINCED

1 TEASPOON SUGAR

5 TABLESPOONS RED PEPPER FLAKES

3 BUNCHES SCALLIONS, TRIMMED AND SLICED

WATER, AS NEEDED

DIRECTIONS

1. Place the cabbage and salt in a large bowl and stir to combine. Wash your hands, or put on gloves, and work the mixture with your hands, squeezing to remove as much liquid as possible from the cabbage. Let the mixture rest for 2 hours.

2. Add the ginger, garlic, sugar, red pepper flakes, and scallions, work the mixture with your hands until well combined, and squeeze to remove as much liquid as possible.

3. Transfer the mixture to a large mason jar and press down so it is tightly packed together. The liquid should be covering the mixture. If it is not, add water until the mixture is covered.

4. Cover the jar and let the mixture sit at room temperature for 3 to 7 days, removing the lid daily to release the gas that has built up.

Corn Tortillas

Masa harina is a very fine flour that is made from hominy or corn kernels that have been cooked and soaked in a diluted solution of calcium hydroxide—aka limewater—before being milled.

YIELD: **20 TORTILLAS**

ACTIVE TIME: **30 MINUTES**

TOTAL TIME: **1 HOUR**

INGREDIENTS

2 CUPS MASA HARINA, PLUS MORE AS NEEDED

½ TEASPOON KOSHER SALT

1 CUP WARM WATER (110°F), PLUS MORE AS NEEDED

2 TABLESPOONS VEGETABLE OIL

DIRECTIONS

1. Place the masa harina and salt in a bowl and stir to combine. Slowly add the warm water and oil and stir until they are incorporated and a soft dough forms. The dough should be quite soft and not at all sticky. If it is too dry, add more water. If the dough is too wet, add more masa harina. Wrap the dough in plastic and let it rest at room temperature for 30 minutes. It can also be stored in the refrigerator for up to 24 hours.

2. Warm a cast-iron skillet over medium-high heat. Pinch off a small piece of the dough and roll it into a ball. Place the ball between two pieces of parchment paper or plastic wrap and use a large cookbook (or something of similar weight) to flatten the ball into a thin disk.

3. Place the disk in the skillet and cook until brown spots begin to appear, about 45 seconds. Flip the disk over, cook for 1 minute, and transfer the cooked tortilla to a plate. Cover with a kitchen towel and repeat with the remaining dough.

Dumpling Wrappers

A homemade dumpling is one of the best ways to convey the considerable bounty from your garden to others.

YIELD: **36 WRAPPERS**

ACTIVE TIME: **45 MINUTES**

TOTAL TIME: **2 HOURS AND 45 MINUTES**

INGREDIENTS

¼ CUP WATER, PLUS MORE AS NEEDED

1 LARGE EGG

¾ TEASPOON KOSHER SALT

1½ CUPS ALL-PURPOSE FLOUR, PLUS MORE AS NEEDED

CORNSTARCH, FOR DUSTING

DIRECTIONS

1. Place the water, egg, and salt in a measuring cup and whisk to combine. Place the flour in the bowl of a stand mixer fitted with the paddle attachment. With the mixer running on low speed, add the egg mixture in a steady stream and beat until the dough holds together. Add water or flour in ½-teaspoon increments if the dough is too dry or too wet, respectively. Fit the mixer with the dough hook and knead at medium speed until the dough is soft, smooth, and springs back quickly when pressed with a finger, about 10 minutes. Cover the dough tightly with plastic wrap and let rest for 2 hours.

2. Cut the dough into three even pieces. Working with one piece at a time (cover the others tightly in plastic), shape the dough into a ball. Place the ball of dough on a flour-dusted work surface and roll it out to ½-inch thick. Feed the dough through a pasta maker, adjusting the setting to reduce the thickness with each pass, until the dough is thin enough that you can see your hand through it. Place the sheets on the work surface, roll out to 6 inches long, and place them on a parchment-lined baking sheet.

3. Dust a work surface with cornstarch, place the dough on it, and cut the sheets into as many 4-inch squares or 3-inch rounds as possible. Pile the cut wrappers on top of each other and fill as desired, or cover in plastic wrap and refrigerate for up to 3 days.

CHAPTER 2

STARTERS

The development of flavors that qualify as decadent takes time. And while not all of the dishes in this book will demand your undivided attention, there are some preparations that will keep you in the kitchen for longer than you'd like if you have company. At those times, it helps to have a number of fun and palate-awakening preparations at your fingertips so that you and your guests will see the wait as being worth it.

From flavorful bites like the Stuffed Peppadew Peppers (see page 62) to delightful dumplings such as the Dudhi Kofta (see page 65), these recipes are easy enough to serve as a quick snack or light lunch, tasty enough to transform a simple get-together into a memorable occasion, and elegant enough to carry a dinner party.

Beet Chips

YIELD: **4 SERVINGS**

ACTIVE TIME: **5 MINUTES**

TOTAL TIME: **20 MINUTES**

You may have tried beet chips from the supermarket, but they are quite easy to make at home. In this recipe, you don't even have to enlist a deep fryer.

INGREDIENTS

5 BEETS, PEELED AND SLICED VERY THIN

¼ CUP OLIVE OIL

2 TEASPOONS SEA SALT

DIRECTIONS

1. Preheat the oven to 400°F. Place the beets and olive oil in a bowl and toss until the slices are evenly coated. Place them on parchment-lined baking sheets in a single layer. Bake for 12 to 15 minutes, or until crispy.

2. Remove from the oven, transfer to a bowl, add the salt, and toss to coat. Serve warm or store in an airtight container for up to 1 week.

Herbed Goat Cheese

YIELD: **4 SERVINGS**

ACTIVE TIME: **10 MINUTES**

TOTAL TIME: **1 HOUR AND 10 MINUTES**

Fresh herbs infuse the goat cheese with deliciously vibrant flavors, while still allowing the cheese's tanginess to shine through.

INGREDIENTS

½ LB. GOAT CHEESE

2 TABLESPOONS FINELY CHOPPED FRESH TARRAGON

2 TABLESPOONS FINELY CHOPPED FRESH CHIVES

2 TABLESPOONS FINELY CHOPPED FRESH THYME

1 CUP OLIVE OIL

CRUSTY BREAD, FOR SERVING

CRACKERS, FOR SERVING

DIRECTIONS

1. Slice the goat cheese into thick rounds. Gently roll the rounds in the herbs and gently press down so that the herbs adhere to the surface of the cheese.

2. Layer the rounds in glass jars. Pour olive oil over them until they are covered. Let sit for 1 hour before serving with crusty bread and crackers.

Chili-Lime Taro Fries

YIELD: **4 SERVINGS**

ACTIVE TIME: **15 MINUTES**

TOTAL TIME: **20 MINUTES**

You'll soon see why fried taro is such a popular street food in Thailand.

INGREDIENTS

VEGETABLE OIL, AS NEEDED

1 LARGE TARO ROOT, PEELED AND JULIENNED

SALT, TO TASTE

ANCHO CHILI POWDER, TO TASTE

2 TABLESPOONS FRESH LIME JUICE

DIRECTIONS

1. Add vegetable oil to a Dutch oven until it is 2 or 3 inches deep. Warm to 350°F over medium-high heat.

2. Add the taro root strips and fry until golden brown, about 5 minutes. Make sure not to crowd the pot, working in batches if necessary. Transfer the fries to a large bowl. Sprinkle immediately with the salt and chili powder and drizzle with lime juice.

3. Toss until the seasonings are evenly distributed and serve.

Black Olive Tapenade

YIELD: **1½ CUPS**

ACTIVE TIME: **5 MINUTES**

TOTAL TIME: **5 MINUTES**

This spread can be made with any type of olives, but black olives produce the most aesthetically pleasing result.

INGREDIENTS

1½ CUPS CURED BLACK OLIVES, PITTED

1 TEASPOON WHITE MISO PASTE

3 TABLESPOONS CAPERS, RINSED

1½ TABLESPOONS FINELY CHOPPED FRESH PARSLEY

3 GARLIC CLOVES

3 TABLESPOONS FRESH LEMON JUICE

¼ TEASPOON BLACK PEPPER, PLUS MORE TO TASTE

¼ CUP OLIVE OIL

SALT, TO TASTE

DIRECTIONS

1. Place the olives, miso paste, capers, parsley, garlic, lemon juice, and black pepper in a food processor and pulse until coarsely chopped.

2. Drizzle the olive oil into the mixture and pulse a few more times until a chunky paste forms, scraping down the work bowl as needed. Season with salt and pepper and serve.

White Bean & Rosemary Spread

YIELD: **2 CUPS**

ACTIVE TIME: **5 MINUTES**

TOTAL TIME: **35 MINUTES**

With the addition of a freshly picked sprig of rosemary, this spread can be made with ingredients that one always seems to have at their fingertips.

INGREDIENTS

1 (14 OZ.) CAN CANNELLINI BEANS, DRAINED AND RINSED

2 TABLESPOONS OLIVE OIL

2 TEASPOONS BALSAMIC VINEGAR

2 GARLIC CLOVES, MINCED

1 TABLESPOON FINELY CHOPPED FRESH ROSEMARY

½ CELERY STALK, MINCED

SALT AND PEPPER, TO TASTE

2 PINCHES RED PEPPER FLAKES

CRUDITÉS, FOR SERVING

CRACKERS, FOR SERVING

DIRECTIONS

1. Place half of the beans in a bowl and mash them. Add the rest of the beans, the olive oil, vinegar, garlic, rosemary, and celery and stir to combine.

2. Season with salt, pepper, and red pepper flakes and cover the bowl with plastic wrap. Let stand for about 30 minutes before serving with crudités and crackers.

Spanish Potato Tortilla

YIELD: **6 SERVINGS**

ACTIVE TIME: **30 MINUTES**

TOTAL TIME: **2 HOURS**

Hearty, filling, and easy to master, this is perfect for those days when you and a group of friends will just be milling around the house.

INGREDIENTS

5 LARGE RUSSET POTATOES, PEELED AND SLICED THIN

1 SPANISH ONION, SLICED

½ CUP VEGETABLE OIL, PLUS MORE AS NEEDED

½ CUP OLIVE OIL

10 EGGS, AT ROOM TEMPERATURE

1 GENEROUS PINCH KOSHER SALT

DIRECTIONS

1. Place the potatoes, onion, vegetable oil, and olive oil in a 12-inch cast-iron skillet. The potatoes should be submerged. If not, add more vegetable oil as needed. Bring to a gentle simmer over low heat and cook until the potatoes are tender, about 30 minutes. Remove from heat and let cool slightly.

2. Use a slotted spoon to remove the potatoes and onion from the oil. Reserve the oil. Place the eggs and salt in a large bowl and whisk to combine. Add the potatoes and onion to the eggs.

3. Warm the skillet over high heat. Add ¼ cup of the reserved oil and swirl to coat the bottom and sides of the pan. Pour the egg-and-potato mixture into the pan and stir vigorously to ensure that the mixture does not stick to the sides. Cook for 1 minute and remove from heat. Place the pan over low heat, cover, and cook for 3 minutes.

4. Carefully invert the tortilla onto a large plate. Return it to the skillet, cook for 3 minutes, and then invert it onto the plate. Return it to the skillet and cook for another 3 minutes. Remove the tortilla from the pan and let it rest at room temperature for 1 hour before serving.

Pumpkin Dip

YIELD: **6 TO 8 SERVINGS**

ACTIVE TIME: **5 MINUTES**

TOTAL TIME: **35 MINUTES**

Packaging the sweet, savory flavor of pumpkin in a dip will help sustain you after the warmth of the summer months departs.

INGREDIENTS

1 (3 LB.) SUGAR PUMPKIN, HALVED AND SEEDED

1 TABLESPOON OLIVE OIL

2 TEASPOONS KOSHER SALT

1 TEASPOON BLACK PEPPER

¼ CUP OLIVE OIL

1 TEASPOON FINELY CHOPPED FRESH THYME

¼ TEASPOON GRATED NUTMEG

¼ CUP GRATED PARMESAN CHEESE

1 TABLESPOON FRESH LEMON JUICE

1 TABLESPOON PLAIN GREEK YOGURT

DIRECTIONS

1. Preheat the oven to 425°F. Place the pumpkin, cut-side up, on a parchment-lined baking sheet and brush it with the olive oil. Sprinkle half of the salt over the pumpkin, place it in the oven, and roast for 25 to 30 minutes, until the flesh is tender. Remove from the oven and let the pumpkin cool.

2. When the pumpkin is cool enough to handle, scrape the flesh into a food processor. Add the remaining ingredients and puree until smooth.

Onion Bhaji

YIELD: **4 SERVINGS**

ACTIVE TIME: **20 MINUTES**

TOTAL TIME: **20 MINUTES**

These fritters can be varied in dozens of ways. Try adding shredded carrot, chilies, a bit of coconut, or even grated parsnip to get an idea of what else you might like to incorporate.

INGREDIENTS

2 EGGS

3 LARGE RED ONIONS, SLICED INTO THIN HALF-MOONS

1 CUP ALL-PURPOSE FLOUR

1 TEASPOON CORIANDER

1 TEASPOON CUMIN

1 SERRANO PEPPER, STEMMED, SEEDED, AND MINCED

½ TEASPOON KOSHER SALT

1 CUP VEGETABLE OIL, PLUS MORE AS NEEDED

DIRECTIONS

1. Place the eggs in a bowl and whisk until scrambled. Add the onions, flour, coriander, cumin, serrano pepper, and salt and stir to combine.

2. Place the vegetable oil in an 8-inch cast-iron skillet and warm over medium heat. When it starts to shimmer, add a large spoonful of the onion batter and fry until golden brown, about 30 to 45 seconds.

3. Turn the fritter over and fry until it is crisp and golden brown all over, about 30 seconds. Transfer to a paper towel–lined plate to drain. Repeat with the remaining batter, adding and heating more oil if it starts to run low. When all of the fritters have been cooked, serve immediately.

Stuffed Peppadew Peppers

YIELD: **4 TO 6 SERVINGS**

ACTIVE TIME: **10 MINUTES**

TOTAL TIME: **10 MINUTES**

The peppadew's unique combination of sweet, spicy, and tangy is ideal for the creamy zip provided by goat cheese.

INGREDIENTS

½ LB. GOAT CHEESE

1 (14 OZ.) JAR PEPPADEW PEPPERS

¼ CUP OLIVE OIL

¼ CUP FINELY CHOPPED FRESH BASIL

1 BAGUETTE, SLICED AND TOASTED, FOR SERVING

DIRECTIONS

1. Stir the goat cheese until it has warmed and become spreadable. Spoon it into a piping bag fitted with a fine round tip or a resealable plastic bag with a small hole cut in one corner.

2. Drain the peppadew peppers, but don't rinse them. Pipe the goat cheese into the peppers' cavities and place them on a plate. Drizzle olive oil over the stuffed peppers and sprinkle the basil on top. Serve with the toasted baguette.

Dudhi Kofta

YIELD: **6 SERVINGS**

ACTIVE TIME: **30 MINUTES**

TOTAL TIME: **1 HOUR**

A great way to use up the surplus of zucchini that every summer seems to bring.

INGREDIENTS

2 LBS. ZUCCHINI, TRIMMED AND GRATED

2 TEASPOONS KOSHER SALT

1 SMALL RED ONION, CHOPPED

¼ CUP RAW CASHEWS

2 GARLIC CLOVES, MINCED

1-INCH PIECE FRESH GINGER, PEELED AND MINCED

4 BIRD'S EYE CHILI PEPPERS, STEMMED, SEEDED, AND MINCED

½ CUP CHICKPEA FLOUR

2 TABLESPOONS FINELY CHOPPED FRESH CILANTRO

4 CUPS VEGETABLE OIL

DIRECTIONS

1. Place the grated zucchini in a bowl, add the salt, and stir to combine. Let stand for 20 minutes.

2. Place the onion, cashews, garlic, ginger, and chilies in a food processor and blitz until the mixture becomes a chunky puree.

3. Place the zucchini in a kitchen towel and wring it to remove as much liquid as possible. Place the zucchini in a mixing bowl and add the onion-and-cashew puree. Stir to combine, add the chickpea flour and cilantro, and fold to incorporate. The dough should be slightly wet.

4. Place the vegetable oil in a Dutch oven and heat it to 300°F. As the oil warms, form tablespoons of the dough into balls and place them on a parchment-lined baking sheet. When the oil is ready, place the dumplings in the oil and fry until golden brown, about 5 minutes. Work in batches if necessary. Transfer the cooked dumplings to a paper towel–lined plate to drain.

Muthia with Cilantro Yogurt

YIELD: **6 SERVINGS**

ACTIVE TIME: **20 MINUTES**

TOTAL TIME: **30 MINUTES**

If cabbage isn't your thing, feel free to substitute any leafy green in its place.

INGREDIENTS

FOR THE MUTHIA

1 TABLESPOON KOSHER SALT

1 GREEN CABBAGE, OUTER LEAVES RESERVED, REMAINDER CHOPPED

1½ CUPS CHICKPEA FLOUR, PLUS MORE FOR DUSTING

2 TABLESPOONS COCONUT OIL, MELTED

2-INCH PIECE FRESH GINGER, PEELED AND MINCED

2 TABLESPOONS MINCED FRESNO CHILI PEPPER

1 TABLESPOON CORIANDER

1½ TEASPOONS CUMIN

½ TEASPOON TURMERIC

1½ TEASPOONS KOSHER SALT

FOR THE YOGURT

1 CUP FRESH CILANTRO LEAVES

1 CUP BABY SPINACH

¼ CUP COLD WATER

2 CUPS PLAIN YOGURT

1 PINCH CAYENNE PEPPER

DIRECTIONS

1. To begin preparations for the muthia, fill a Dutch oven with water, add the salt, and bring to a boil. Prepare an ice water bath as the water warms. Add the chopped cabbage to the boiling water and cook for 1 minute. Use a strainer to transfer the cabbage to the ice water bath. Drain and squeeze the cabbage to remove any excess liquid. Place on a kitchen towel to dry. Keep the water in the Dutch oven.

2. Place the chickpea flour and coconut oil in a bowl and stir to combine. Add the cabbage and the remaining ingredients and stir until the dough starts to hold together. Place the dough on a flour-dusted work surface and knead until it is smooth and stiff. Divide and roll the dough into 18 balls.

3. Place 1 inch of water in a large pot and place a steaming tray in the pot. Line the steaming tray with the reserved cabbage leaves and place the dumplings on top. Bring the water to a boil and steam the dumplings until they are shiny and firm, about 20 minutes.

4. While the dumplings are steaming, prepare the yogurt. Bring the water in the Dutch oven back to a boil and prepare another ice water bath. Add the cilantro and spinach to the boiling water, cook for 1 minute, drain, and transfer the cilantro and spinach to the ice water bath. Drain, squeeze to remove as much liquid from the mixture as possible, and transfer the mixture to a food processor. Add the water and half of the yogurt to the food processor and puree until smooth. Place this mixture, the cayenne pepper, and the remaining yogurt in a bowl, stir to combine, and serve alongside the steamed dumplings.

Punjabi Samosa

YIELD: **16 SAMOSA**

ACTIVE TIME: **45 MINUTES**

TOTAL TIME: **1 HOUR AND 30 MINUTES**

Maida flour is finely milled to remove all of the bran from the wheat, producing a soft result that closely resembles cake flour.

INGREDIENTS

FOR THE WRAPPERS

2 CUPS MAIDA FLOUR, PLUS MORE FOR DUSTING

¼ TEASPOON KOSHER SALT

2 TABLESPOONS OLIVE OIL

½ CUP WATER, PLUS MORE AS NEEDED

FOR THE FILLING

2 RUSSET POTATOES, PEELED AND CHOPPED

2 TABLESPOONS VEGETABLE OIL, PLUS MORE AS NEEDED

1 TEASPOON CORIANDER SEEDS, CRUSHED

½ TEASPOON FENNEL SEEDS, CRUSHED

1 PINCH FENUGREEK SEEDS, CRUSHED

1-INCH PIECE FRESH GINGER, PEELED AND MINCED

Continued...

DIRECTIONS

1. To begin preparations for the wrappers, place the flour and salt in a mixing bowl and use your hands to combine. Add the oil and work the mixture with your hands until it is a coarse meal. Add the water and knead the mixture until a smooth, firm dough forms. If the dough is too dry, incorporate more water, adding 1 tablespoon at a time. Cover the bowl with a kitchen towel and set aside.

2. To begin preparations for the filling, place the potatoes in a saucepan and cover with water. Bring the water to a boil and cook until fork-tender, about 20 minutes. Transfer to a bowl, mash until smooth, and set aside.

3. Place the oil in a skillet and warm over medium heat. Add the crushed seeds and cook until fragrant, about 2 minutes. Add the ginger, garlic, and jalapeño, stir-fry for 2 minutes, and then add the chili powder, coriander, turmeric, amchoor powder, and garam masala. Cook for another minute before adding the mashed potatoes and the curry leaves. Stir to combine, season with salt, transfer the mixture to a bowl, and let it cool completely.

4. Divide the dough for the wrappers into eight pieces and roll each one out into a 6-inch circle on a flour-dusted work surface. Cut the circles in half and brush the flat edge of each

Continued...

1 GARLIC CLOVE, MINCED

1 TEASPOON MINCED JALAPEÑO PEPPER

2 TEASPOONS CHILI POWDER

2 TABLESPOONS CORIANDER

¾ TEASPOON TURMERIC

1 TABLESPOON AMCHOOR POWDER

½ TEASPOON GARAM MASALA

6 CURRY LEAVES, MINCED

SALT, TO TASTE

piece with water. Fold one corner of the flat edge toward the other to make a cone and pinch to seal. Fill each cone one-third of the way with the filling, brush the opening with water, and pinch to seal. Place the sealed samosas on a parchment-lined baking sheet.

5. Add vegetable oil to a Dutch oven until it is 3 inches deep and heat it to 325°F. Working in batches, add the filled samosas to the hot oil and fry, turning them as they cook, until they are golden brown, about 5 minutes. Transfer the cooked samosas to a paper towel–lined plate and serve once they have all been cooked.

Shiitake Siu Mai

YIELD: **6 TO 8 SERVINGS**

ACTIVE TIME: **25 MINUTES**

TOTAL TIME: **45 MINUTES**

This sweet-and-savory filling will even satisfy the dim sum purist who feels the flavor provided by the pork is essential.

INGREDIENTS

8 SHIITAKE MUSHROOM CAPS, MINCED

4 SCALLIONS, TRIMMED AND SLICED THIN

¼ RED BELL PEPPER, SEEDED AND MINCED

¼ CUP RAISINS

¼ CUP PINE NUTS, TOASTED

¼ CUP CORN KERNELS

1 TABLESPOON SOY SAUCE, PLUS MORE FOR SERVING

1 TABLESPOON SHAOXING RICE WINE

1 TEASPOON TOASTED SESAME OIL

2 TEASPOONS CORNSTARCH

½ TEASPOON SUGAR

½ TEASPOON WHITE PEPPER

36 ROUND DUMPLING WRAPPERS (SEE PAGE 43)

CABBAGE LEAVES, FOR STEAMING

CARROTS, PEELED AND MINCED, FOR GARNISH

DIRECTIONS

1. Place all of the ingredients, except for the wrappers, cabbage leaves, and carrots, in a mixing bowl and stir until well combined.

2. Place a wrapper in a cupped hand and fill with enough of the mixture to fill the wrapper to the top. Flatten the filling with a butter knife and gently tighten the wrapper around the filling, forming a rough cylindrical shape with a flat bottom. Place the filled dumplings on a parchment-lined baking sheet and repeat with the remaining wrappers and filling.

3. Place 1 inch of water in a large pot and bring it to a boil. Line a steaming tray with the cabbage leaves and then add the siu mai, leaving ½ inch between each of the dumplings and also between the dumplings and the edge of the tray. Place the steaming tray over the boiling water, cover, and steam until the dumplings are cooked through, tender, and still chewy, about 10 minutes. Transfer the cooked dumplings to a warmed platter, garnish with the carrots, and serve with additional soy sauce.

Vegetarian Empanadas

Achiote is a vibrant, reddish orange spice that is made from ground annatto seeds, and its nutty, sweet, and earthy flavor is the key to these delectable pockets.

YIELD: **4 SERVINGS**

ACTIVE TIME: **30 MINUTES**

TOTAL TIME: **1 HOUR**

INGREDIENTS

FOR THE DOUGH

¼ TEASPOON KOSHER SALT

6 TABLESPOONS WARM WATER (110°F)

1½ CUPS ALL-PURPOSE FLOUR, PLUS MORE FOR DUSTING

3 TABLESPOONS UNSALTED BUTTER, CUT INTO SMALL PIECES

FOR THE FILLING

2 TEASPOONS VEGETABLE OIL, PLUS MORE AS NEEDED

1 YELLOW ONION, MINCED

1 CUP SHREDDED NAPA CABBAGE

2 CARROTS, PEELED AND GRATED

1 GARLIC CLOVE, MINCED

1 (14 OZ.) CAN DICED TOMATOES

½ TEASPOON KOSHER SALT

¼ TEASPOON BLACK PEPPER

½ TEASPOON ACHIOTE

½ TEASPOON CUMIN

CHILI POWDER, TO TASTE

DIRECTIONS

1. To prepare the dough, dissolve the salt in the warm water. Place the flour in a mixing bowl, add the butter, and work the mixture with a pastry blender until it is coarse crumbs. Add the salted water and knead the mixture until a stiff dough forms. Cut the dough into eight pieces, cover them with plastic wrap, and place in the refrigerator for 20 minutes.

2. To prepare the filling, place the vegetable oil in a skillet and warm over medium heat. Add the onion, cabbage, and carrots and cook until soft, about 10 minutes. Add the garlic, cook until fragrant, about 2 minutes, and then transfer the mixture to a mixing bowl. Add the tomatoes and seasonings, stir to combine, and let the mixture cool completely.

3. Add vegetable oil to a Dutch oven until it is 3 inches deep and bring it to 350°F. Preheat the oven to 200°F and place a baking sheet in the oven. Place the dough on a flour-dusted work surface and roll each piece into a 5-inch circle. Place 3 tablespoons of the filling in the center of a circle, brush the edge with water, and fold into a half-moon. Press down on the edge to seal the empanada tight, trying to remove as much air as possible. Repeat with the remaining pieces of dough and filling.

4. Working in two batches, place the empanadas in the hot oil and fry until golden brown, about 5 minutes. Drain on paper towels and place them on the baking sheet in the warm oven while you cook the next batch.

INGREDIENTS

FOR THE WRAPPERS

1 CUP WHEAT STARCH, PLUS MORE
FOR DUSTING

½ CUP CORNSTARCH

1¼ CUPS BOILING WATER

1 TABLESPOON GRAPESEED OR
SAFFLOWER OIL

FOR THE FILLING

2 TABLESPOONS PEANUT OIL

1 LB. JICAMA, PEELED AND GRATED

¼ CUP MINCED SHIITAKE
MUSHROOM CAPS

1 CARROT, PEELED AND GRATED

2 TABLESPOONS SOY SAUCE

1 TEASPOON SUGAR

SALT AND PEPPER, TO TASTE

CABBAGE LEAVES, FOR STEAMING

CHILI GARLIC SAUCE, FOR SERVING

Chai Kuih

YIELD: **4 SERVINGS**

ACTIVE TIME: **1 HOUR**

TOTAL TIME: **2 HOURS**

These "vegetable cakes" are a popular street food in a number of Chinese cities.

DIRECTIONS

1. To begin preparations for the wrappers, cut a resealable plastic bag at the seams so that you have two squares of plastic and set aside. Place the wheat starch and cornstarch in a heatproof medium bowl. Add the boiling water and oil. Using a rubber spatula, stir the ingredients until a loose dough forms. Turn the dough out onto a work surface dusted with wheat starch and knead until it is smooth and slowly bounces back into place when pressed with a finger. This should take about 10 minutes.

2. Roll out the dough into a 1½-inch-thick log. Cut it into 18 equal pieces, dust them with wheat starch, and cover with plastic wrap. Press down lightly on the pieces to create a disk that is roughly ¼ inch thick. Place the disks between the two squares of plastic and press down with a rolling pin until ⅛ inch thick. Dredge any disks that feel sticky with wheat starch and place them on a parchment-lined baking sheet.

3. To prepare the filling, place the oil in a wok or large skillet and warm over low heat. When the oil begins to shimmer, add the jicama, mushrooms, and carrot and cook, stirring frequently, until the jicama is tender but still crunchy, about 15 minutes. Add the soy sauce and sugar, season with salt and pepper, and stir to combine. Remove from heat and let the mixture cool.

4. Place 1 tablespoon of the filling in the center of a wrapper. Moisten the wrapper's edge with a wet finger and fold the wrapper over to create a triangle. Take the far edge of the wrapper and gently fold it over the filling to meet the other edge. Using your thumb and index finger, pinch both edges together to create a tight seal, while pressing down to remove as much air as you can.

5. Place 1 inch of water in a saucepan and bring it to a boil. Line a steaming tray with the cabbage leaves and place the dumplings in the tray, leaving ½ inch between each of the dumplings and also between the dumplings and the edge of the tray. Place the tray over the boiling water, cover, and steam until the dumplings are tender but still chewy, about 10 minutes. Transfer the dumplings to a warmed platter and serve immediately, accompanied by chili garlic sauce.

Tofu-Filled Momos

Pressed tofu gives body to the filling in these classic vegetarian dumplings.

YIELD: **4 TO 6 SERVINGS**

ACTIVE TIME: **1 HOUR**

TOTAL TIME: **1 HOUR AND 30 MINUTES**

INGREDIENTS

8 DRIED SHIITAKE MUSHROOMS, RECONSTITUTED AND CHOPPED

SALT, TO TASTE

½ LB. PRESSED TOFU, DICED

1 LB. FROZEN SPINACH

6 SCALLIONS, TRIMMED AND SLICED THIN

2 HANDFULS FRESH CILANTRO LEAVES

3 GARLIC CLOVES, MINCED

2-INCH PIECE FRESH GINGER, PEELED AND MINCED

2 CARROTS, PEELED AND GRATED

3 TABLESPOONS SOY SAUCE

36 ROUND DUMPLING WRAPPERS (SEE PAGE 43)

CABBAGE LEAVES, FOR STEAMING

DIRECTIONS

1. Place the mushrooms in a food processor, add a pinch of salt, and pulse 3 or 4 times. Add the tofu, spinach, scallions, cilantro, and another pinch of salt and pulse until the mixture is finely chopped. Add the garlic and ginger and pulse until incorporated.

2. Transfer the mixture to a medium bowl. Add the carrots and soy sauce and mix until thoroughly combined. Take a small bit of the mixture, form into a patty, and fry in a small skillet. Taste and adjust the seasoning as needed.

3. Place a damp paper towel over the stack of wrappers to keep them from drying out. Line a baking sheet with parchment paper and set aside a small bowl of water for sealing.

4. Place a wrapper in a cupped hand and put about 1 tablespoon of filling in the center, leaving about ½ inch of the wrapper clear all the way around. Lightly moisten that edge, fold one edge of the wrapper over the filling to form a half-moon, and tightly press the edges together to seal, pressing down to remove as much air as you can as you do it. To pleat the sealed edges, start at one end of the half-moon and make small folds in the wrapper, pressing them flat as you work your way along the edge, making seven to eight folds per dumpling. Repeat with the remaining wrappers and filling.

Continued...

5. Bring 1 cup of water to a boil in a large pot. Line a steaming tray with cabbage leaves. Working in batches, set the momos in the steaming tray, leaving ½ inch between the momos and between the momos and the sides of the steaming tray. Place the steaming tray over the boiling water, cover, and steam until they have puffed out slightly and become slightly translucent, about 12 minutes. Transfer to a warmed plate and tent loosely with aluminum foil to keep warm. Serve immediately once all of the dumplings have been cooked.

Zucchini Fritters

YIELD: **4 SERVINGS**

ACTIVE TIME: **15 MINUTES**

TOTAL TIME: **1 HOUR AND 30 MINUTES**

Zucchini has a number of wonderful uses, and turning it into fritters is one of the easiest ways to get people excited about it.

INGREDIENTS

1½ LBS. ZUCCHINI

SALT AND PEPPER, TO TASTE

¼ CUP ALL-PURPOSE FLOUR

¼ CUP GRATED PARMESAN CHEESE

1 EGG, BEATEN

3 TABLESPOONS OLIVE OIL

DIRECTIONS

1. Line a colander with cheesecloth and grate the zucchini into the colander. Generously sprinkle salt over the zucchini, stir to combine, and let sit for 1 hour. After 1 hour, press down on the zucchini to remove as much liquid from it as you can.

2. Place the zucchini, flour, Parmesan, and egg in a mixing bowl and stir to combine. Use your hands to form handfuls of the mixture into balls and then gently press down on the balls to flatten them into patties.

3. Place the oil in a cast-iron skillet and warm over medium-high heat. Working in batches, place the patties into the oil, taking care not to crowd the skillet. Cook until golden brown, about 5 minutes. Flip them over and cook for another 5 minutes, until the fritters are also golden brown on that side. Remove from the skillet, transfer to a paper towel–lined plate, and repeat with the remaining patties. When all of the fritters have been cooked, season with salt and pepper and serve.

Roman-Style Artichokes

YIELD: **2 TO 4 SERVINGS**

ACTIVE TIME: **20 MINUTES**

TOTAL TIME: **30 MINUTES**

When fried, artichoke hearts need nothing more than a squeeze of lemon juice to shine. This simple lemony mayonnaise makes them irresistible.

INGREDIENTS

2 LARGE ARTICHOKES

1 LEMON, QUARTERED

VEGETABLE OIL, AS NEEDED

SALT, TO TASTE

LEMON-PEPPER MAYONNAISE (SEE SIDEBAR), FOR SERVING

DIRECTIONS

1. Prepare the artichokes by using a serrated knife to cut off the top half with the leaves and all but the last inch of the stem; continue whittling away the outer leaves until you see the hairy-looking choke within.

2. Using a paring knife, peel the outer layer of the remaining part of the stem; cut the remaining artichoke into quarters and remove the hairy part in the middle. You should have the heart with a little bit of lower leaves left. Place in a bowl of water, add a squeeze of lemon juice, and set aside.

3. Bring water to a boil in a small saucepan. Add the artichokes and parboil until they begin to feel tender, about 3 to 5 minutes. Remove from the water and drain.

4. Place another small pot on the stove and fill with enough oil that the artichoke hearts will be submerged. Warm the oil over medium heat until it starts to sizzle.

5. Place the artichokes in the oil and fry until they are brown all over, turning occasionally, 8 to 10 minutes. Transfer to a paper towel-lined plate to drain and let cool. Sprinkle with salt and serve with the lemon wedges and the Lemon-Pepper Mayonnaise.

LEMON-PEPPER MAYONNAISE

Place 1 cup mayonnaise, 3 tablespoons grated Parmesan cheese, 1 tablespoon lemon zest, 3 tablespoons fresh lemon juice, 1½ teaspoons black pepper, and 2 teaspoons kosher salt in a mixing bowl and whisk until combined.

CHAPTER 3

SALADS

The carnivore-centric construction of most restaurant menus means that every vegetarian is well acquainted with the concept of salad. In terms of flexibility, freshness, and speed, a salad is unmatched. But too often a lack of inspiration and imagination turn salad into a slightly depressing option that feels something like a concession of defeat.

Despite that reputation, a salad can be one of the most important tools in a bold cook's repertoire, creating a safe space for flavor experiments and enabling one to significantly cut down on waste. With that in mind, the salads in this section intend to revive your passion, offering inventive options and an array of delicious dressings and vinaigrettes that will remove salad from its default position for good.

Spring Salad with Green Goddess Dressing

YIELD: **4 SERVINGS**

ACTIVE TIME: **15 MINUTES**

TOTAL TIME: **15 MINUTES**

The divine moniker is no accident—this dressing is thick and robust enough to lend body to this light salad, but delicate enough to keep you mindful of the fresh herbs that produced it.

INGREDIENTS

FOR THE DRESSING

½ CUP MAYONNAISE

⅔ CUP BUTTERMILK

1 TABLESPOON FRESH LEMON JUICE

2 TABLESPOONS CHOPPED CELERY LEAVES

2 TABLESPOONS CHOPPED FRESH PARSLEY LEAVES

2 TABLESPOONS CHOPPED FRESH TARRAGON

2 TABLESPOONS CHOPPED FRESH CHIVES

2 TEASPOONS KOSHER SALT

1 TEASPOON BLACK PEPPER

FOR THE SALAD

SALT AND PEPPER, TO TASTE

6 ASPARAGUS STALKS, TRIMMED AND CHOPPED

4 OZ. SNAP PEAS, TRIMMED AND CHOPPED

3 HEADS BABY RED LEAF LETTUCE, HALVED

3 RADISHES, SLICED THIN WITH A MANDOLINE, FOR GARNISH

CELERY LEAVES, FOR GARNISH

DIRECTIONS

1. To prepare the dressing, place all of the ingredients in a food processor and puree until thoroughly combined. Transfer to a container and place in the refrigerator until ready to serve.

2. To begin preparations for the salad, bring a pot of salted water to a boil and prepare an ice water bath in a large bowl. Place the asparagus in the boiling water, cook for 1 minute, remove with a strainer, and transfer to the water bath until completely cool. Transfer to a kitchen towel to dry.

3. Place the peas in the boiling water, cook for 1 minute, remove with a strainer, and transfer to the water bath until completely cool. Transfer to a kitchen towel to dry.

4. Place the halved heads of lettuce on the serving plates. Place the asparagus and peas in a bowl, season with salt and pepper, and add half of the dressing. Toss to combine and place the mixture on top of the lettuce. Drizzle with additional dressing and garnish with the radishes and celery leaves.

Peppers Stuffed with Greek Salad

YIELD: **4 SERVINGS**

ACTIVE TIME: **10 MINUTES**

TOTAL TIME: **25 MINUTES**

The peppers are not essential, but they add a lovely element to the presentation and balance out the savory feta with their fresh taste.

INGREDIENTS

4 YELLOW BELL PEPPERS, SEEDED AND HALVED

12 CHERRY TOMATOES, HALVED

2 GARLIC CLOVES, MINCED

2 TABLESPOONS OLIVE OIL

½ CUP CRUMBLED FETA CHEESE

1 CUP BLACK OLIVES, PITTED

SALT AND PEPPER, TO TASTE

LEAVES FROM 1 BUNCH FRESH BASIL

DIRECTIONS

1. Preheat the oven to 375°F and place the peppers on a parchment-lined baking sheet.

2. Place the cherry tomatoes, garlic, olive oil, feta, and black olives in a mixing bowl and stir to combine. Divide the mixture between the peppers, place them in the oven, and roast until the peppers start to collapse, 10 to 15 minutes.

3. Remove the peppers from the oven and let cool slightly. Season with salt and pepper and top with the basil leaves before serving.

Panzanella with White Balsamic Vinaigrette

YIELD: **6 SERVINGS**

ACTIVE TIME: **20 MINUTES**

TOTAL TIME: **40 MINUTES**

When caught in the breakneck pace of the summer, quick dishes that can salvage ingredients that have lingered slightly too long are extremely valuable. This salad is one such treasure.

INGREDIENTS

FOR THE SALAD

1 TABLESPOON KOSHER SALT, PLUS 2 TEASPOONS

6 PEARL ONIONS, TRIMMED

1 CUP CORN KERNELS

1 CUP CHOPPED GREEN BEANS

4 CUPS CHOPPED DAY-OLD BREAD

2 CUPS CHOPPED OVERRIPE TOMATOES

10 LARGE FRESH BASIL LEAVES, TORN

BLACK PEPPER, TO TASTE

FOR THE VINAIGRETTE

½ CUP WHITE BALSAMIC VINEGAR

¼ CUP OLIVE OIL

2 TABLESPOONS MINCED SHALLOT

¼ CUP SLICED SCALLIONS

2 TABLESPOONS FINELY CHOPPED FRESH PARSLEY

2 TEASPOONS KOSHER SALT

1 TEASPOON BLACK PEPPER

DIRECTIONS

1. To begin preparations for the salad, bring water to a boil in a small saucepan and prepare an ice water bath. When the water is boiling, add the 1 tablespoon of salt and the pearl onions and cook for 5 minutes. When the onions have 1 minute left to cook, add the corn and green beans to the saucepan. Transfer the vegetables to the ice water bath and let cool completely.

2. Remove the pearl onions from the water bath and squeeze to remove the bulbs from their skins. Cut the bulbs in half and break them down into individual petals. Drain the corn and green beans and pat the vegetables dry.

3. To prepare the vinaigrette, place all of the ingredients in a mixing bowl and whisk until combined.

4. Place the cooked vegetables, bread, tomatoes, and basil in a salad bowl and toss to combine. Add the remaining salt, season with pepper, and add half of the vinaigrette. Toss to coat, taste, and add more of the vinaigrette if desired.

INGREDIENTS

FOR THE SALAD

1 PINT CHERRY TOMATOES

1 TABLESPOON OLIVE OIL

5 GARLIC CLOVES, CRUSHED

LEAVES FROM 2 SPRIGS FRESH THYME

½ TEASPOON KOSHER SALT, PLUS MORE TO TASTE

¼ TEASPOON BLACK PEPPER, PLUS MORE TO TASTE

3 ZUCCHINI, SLICED THIN WITH A MANDOLINE

2 SUMMER SQUASH, SLICED THIN WITH A MANDOLINE

1 RED BELL PEPPER, STEMMED, SEEDED, AND SLICED THIN WITH A MANDOLINE

FOR THE VINAIGRETTE

1 TABLESPOON SLICED FRESH CHIVES

1 TEASPOON FINELY CHOPPED FRESH THYME

1 TEASPOON FINELY CHOPPED FRESH OREGANO

1 TABLESPOON FINELY CHOPPED FRESH PARSLEY

3 TABLESPOONS APPLE CIDER VINEGAR

1 TABLESPOON HONEY

2 TEASPOONS DICED SHALLOT

1 TEASPOON KOSHER SALT

¼ TEASPOON BLACK PEPPER

¼ CUP OLIVE OIL

Shaved Squash Salad with Herb Vinaigrette

YIELD: **4 TO 6 SERVINGS**

ACTIVE TIME: **15 MINUTES**

TOTAL TIME: **40 MINUTES**

Shaved squash and a fresh-tasting vinaigrette make this salad a graceful opening to a special meal.

DIRECTIONS

1. To begin preparations for the salad, preheat the broiler to high. Place the cherry tomatoes, olive oil, garlic, thyme, salt, and pepper in a mixing bowl and toss until the tomatoes are evenly coated. Place the tomatoes on a baking sheet, place in the oven, and broil until the skins begin to burst, 6 to 8 minutes. Remove from the oven and let cool completely.

2. To prepare the vinaigrette, place all of the ingredients, except for the olive oil, in a mixing bowl and whisk to combine. Add the oil in a slow stream while whisking to incorporate. Season to taste and set aside.

3. Place the zucchini, squash, and pepper in a large mixing bowl, season with salt and pepper, and add the vinaigrette. Toss to evenly coat, plate the salad, and sprinkle the blistered tomatoes over the top.

Charred Brassicas with Buttermilk Dressing

YIELD: **4 SERVINGS**

ACTIVE TIME: **20 MINUTES**

TOTAL TIME: **45 MINUTES**

Charring brassicas brings out their sweet side, which pairs wonderfully with the creamy and slightly acidic buttermilk dressing.

INGREDIENTS

FOR THE SALAD

1 SMALL HEAD CAULIFLOWER, CUT INTO BITE-SIZED PIECES

1 HEAD BROCCOLI, CUT INTO FLORETS

¼ CUP OLIVE OIL

4 OZ. BRUSSELS SPROUTS, TRIMMED AND HALVED

SALT AND PEPPER, TO TASTE

PICKLED RAMPS (SEE SIDEBAR)

RED PEPPER FLAKES, FOR GARNISH

PARMESAN CHEESE, GRATED, FOR GARNISH

FOR THE DRESSING

1 LARGE GARLIC CLOVE, MINCED

1 TEASPOON WHITE MISO PASTE

⅔ CUP MAYONNAISE

¼ CUP BUTTERMILK

¼ CUP GRATED PARMESAN CHEESE

ZEST OF 1 LEMON

1 TEASPOON VEGAN WORCESTERSHIRE SAUCE (SEE PAGE 31)

1 TEASPOON KOSHER SALT

½ TEASPOON BLACK PEPPER

DIRECTIONS

1. To begin preparations for the salad, bring a large pot of water to a boil. Add the cauliflower, cook for 1 minute, remove with a slotted spoon, and transfer to a paper towel–lined plate. Wait for the water to return to a boil, add the broccoli, and cook for 30 seconds. Use a slotted spoon to remove the broccoli and let the water drip off before transferring it to the paper towel–lined plate.

2. Place the oil and Brussels sprouts, cut-side down, in a large cast-iron skillet. Add the broccoli and cauliflower, season with salt and pepper, and cook over high heat without moving the vegetables. Cook until charred, turn over, and cook until charred on that side. Remove and transfer to a salad bowl.

3. To prepare the dressing, place all of the ingredients in a food processor and puree until combined. Season to taste.

4. Add the Pickled Ramps and dressing to the salad bowl and toss to evenly coat. Garnish with additional Parmesan cheese and red pepper flakes and serve.

PICKLED RAMPS

Place ½ cup champagne vinegar, ½ cup water, ¼ cup sugar, 1½ teaspoons kosher salt, ¼ teaspoon fennel seeds, ¼ teaspoon coriander seeds, and ⅛ teaspoon red pepper flakes in a small saucepan and bring to a boil. Add 10 small ramp bulbs, reduce heat, and simmer for 1 minute. Transfer the contents of the saucepan to a mason jar, cover, and let cool completely before serving. The ramps will keep in the refrigerator for up to 1 week.

Chilled Corn Salad

YIELD: **4 SERVINGS**

ACTIVE TIME: **15 MINUTES**

TOTAL TIME: **24 HOURS**

This recipe is a riff on a classic Mexican dish known as esquites, *and it can easily be altered to suit your taste and the changing seasons.*

INGREDIENTS

4 CUPS FRESH CORN KERNELS

2 TABLESPOONS UNSALTED BUTTER

1 JALAPEÑO PEPPER, STEMMED, SEEDED, AND DICED

2 TABLESPOONS MAYONNAISE

2 TEASPOONS GARLIC POWDER

3 TABLESPOONS SOUR CREAM

¼ TEASPOON CAYENNE PEPPER

¼ TEASPOON CHILI POWDER

2 TABLESPOONS FETA CHEESE

2 TABLESPOONS COTIJA CHEESE

2 TEASPOONS FRESH LIME JUICE

½ CUP FINELY CHOPPED FRESH CILANTRO

SALT AND PEPPER, TO TASTE

4 CUPS LETTUCE OR ARUGULA

DIRECTIONS

1. Preheat the oven to 400°F. Place the corn on a baking sheet, place it in the oven, and roast until the corn turns a light golden brown, about 35 minutes.

2. Remove the corn from the oven, let cool slightly, and then transfer to a large mixing bowl. Add all of the remaining ingredients, except for the lettuce or arugula, and stir to combine.

3. Place the salad in the refrigerator and refrigerate overnight. When ready to serve, add the lettuce or arugula and stir to incorporate.

   NOTE: If using canned, rather than fresh corn, you can skip roasting the kernels if you choose. If you want to roast them anyway, keep an eye on them after about 15 minutes, as they will not take nearly as long to cook.

Roasted Baby Beet Salad with Blue Cheese Mousse

YIELD: **4 SERVINGS**

ACTIVE TIME: **40 MINUTES**

TOTAL TIME: **1 HOUR AND 45 MINUTES**

When you're working with something as uniquely delicious as baby beets, it's important to keep it simple, and roasting them with a few aromatics accomplishes just that.

INGREDIENTS

FOR THE SALAD

9 BABY BEETS (3 EACH OF RED, GOLDEN, AND PINK)

3 TABLESPOONS OLIVE OIL

1 TABLESPOON KOSHER SALT, PLUS MORE TO TASTE

9 SPRIGS FRESH THYME, LEAVES REMOVED FROM 3

6 GARLIC CLOVES

6 TABLESPOONS WATER

8 RADISHES WITH TOPS

6 OZ. BLUE CHEESE

½ CUP HEAVY CREAM

½ CUP RICOTTA CHEESE

2 APPLES, PEELED, CORED, AND DICED

BLACK PEPPER, TO TASTE

4 PIECES HONEYCOMB, FOR GARNISH

Continued…

DIRECTIONS

1. To begin preparations for the salad, preheat the oven to 400°F. Form three sheets of aluminum foil into pouches. Group the beets according to color and place each group into a pouch. Drizzle each group with the olive oil and sprinkle with salt. Divide the whole sprigs of thyme, the garlic, and water between the pouches and seal them. Place the pouches on a baking sheet, place in the oven, and roast until the beets are fork-tender, 45 minutes to 1 hour depending on the size of the beets. Remove the pouches from the oven and let cool. When cool enough to handle, peel the beets, cut into bite-sized pieces, and set aside.

2. Bring a pot of salted water to a boil and prepare an ice water bath. Remove the greens from the radishes, wash them thoroughly, and set aside. Quarter the radishes.

3. Place the radishes in the boiling water, cook for 1 minute, and then transfer to the ice water bath.

4. Place the blue cheese, heavy cream, ricotta, and thyme leaves in a food processor and puree until smooth. Set the mousse aside.

5. To prepare the vinaigrette, place all of the ingredients, except for the oil, in a small mixing bowl and whisk to combine. Add the oil in a slow stream and whisk until incorporated.

Continued…

FOR THE VINAIGRETTE

¼ CUP HONEY

2 TABLESPOONS WHOLE-GRAIN
MUSTARD

3 TABLESPOONS APPLE CIDER
VINEGAR

1 TEASPOON KOSHER SALT

½ TEASPOON BLACK PEPPER

⅓ CUP OLIVE OIL

6. Place the beets, except for the red variety, in a salad bowl.
    Add the radishes, radish greens, and apples and toss to
    combine. Add half of the vinaigrette, season with salt and
    pepper, and toss to evenly coat.

7. Spread the mousse on the serving dishes. Place salad on
    top, sprinkle the red beets over the salad, drizzle with the
    remaining vinaigrette, and garnish each portion with a piece
    of honeycomb.

Late Summer Salad with Wild Mushrooms, Parmesan & Pine Nuts

YIELD: **4 SERVINGS**

ACTIVE TIME: **25 MINUTES**

TOTAL TIME: **35 MINUTES**

Something about the flavor of this salad makes the late summer light just a bit more golden.

INGREDIENTS

½ CUP OLIVE OIL, PLUS MORE AS NEEDED

½ LB. MUSHROOMS, SLICED

SALT, TO TASTE

¼ CUP DICED RED ONION

1 GARLIC CLOVE, MINCED

¼ CUP BALSAMIC VINEGAR

1 TABLESPOON PINE NUTS

MESCLUN SALAD GREENS, AS NEEDED

2 TABLESPOONS GRATED PARMESAN CHEESE

FRESH DILL, FINELY CHOPPED, TO TASTE

DIRECTIONS

1. Place a few tablespoons of oil in a large skillet and warm over medium-high heat. When the oil starts to shimmer, add the mushrooms, making sure not to crowd the pan. Sprinkle a pinch of salt over the mushrooms as they cook but leave them undisturbed until they release excess water and begin to brown. Gently turn them over to sear the other side. When this side is well browned, transfer to a small bowl.

2. Add the onion, garlic, and, if the pan looks dry, a splash of oil. Sauté over medium heat until the onion starts to soften, about 5 minutes. Turn off heat and deglaze the pan with the balsamic vinegar, scraping up any browned bits from the bottom of the pan. Let the pan cool to room temperature.

3. Place the pine nuts in a small skillet and toast over medium heat for a few minutes, being careful not to burn them. Transfer them to a small bowl or dish and let cool.

4. Place the cooled onion mixture in a bowl and add the ½ cup olive oil. Whisk until combined and season to taste.

5. Arrange the greens on plates and top each portion with the mushrooms, pine nuts, and a light sprinkling of Parmesan and dill. Top with the onion-and-olive oil mixture and serve.

Red & Green Cabbage Salad with Ginger & Tahini Dressing

YIELD: **2 SERVINGS**

ACTIVE TIME: **15 MINUTES**

TOTAL TIME: **15 MINUTES**

The zesty tahini dressing pairs wonderfully with the cabbage, and the ginger ties it all together.

INGREDIENTS

2 CUPS SHREDDED GREEN CABBAGE

2 CUPS SHREDDED RED CABBAGE

3 TABLESPOONS CHOPPED PEANUTS

3 SCALLIONS, TRIMMED AND CHOPPED

½ CUP FINELY CHOPPED FRESH CILANTRO OR PARSLEY

TAHINI DRESSING (SEE PAGE 20)

1 TEASPOON MAPLE SYRUP

1 TEASPOON GRATED FRESH GINGER

1 TEASPOON RICE VINEGAR

1 TEASPOON TOASTED SESAME OIL

½ CUP OLIVE OIL

DIRECTIONS

1. Place the cabbages, peanuts, scallions, and cilantro or parsley in a salad bowl and toss to combine.

2. Place the remaining ingredients in a separate bowl and whisk vigorously until emulsified.

3. Add about ¼ cup of the dressing to the salad and toss. Taste and add more dressing if desired.

INGREDIENTS

FOR THE SALAD

1 (14 OZ.) CAN CHICKPEAS, DRAINED AND RINSED

3 CUPS CAULIFLOWER FLORETS

3 GARLIC CLOVES, SLICED THIN

1 SHALLOT, SLICED THIN

⅓ CUP OLIVE OIL

½ TEASPOON DARK CHILI POWDER

½ TEASPOON CHIPOTLE POWDER

½ TEASPOON BLACK PEPPER

½ TEASPOON ONION POWDER

½ TEASPOON GARLIC POWDER

¼ TEASPOON PAPRIKA

1 TABLESPOON KOSHER SALT

FOR THE DRESSING

2 SCALLIONS, TRIMMED AND SLICED THIN

2 FRESNO CHILI PEPPERS, STEMMED, SEEDED, AND SLICED THIN

3 TABLESPOONS SUGAR

¼ CUP RED WINE VINEGAR

½ TEASPOON DARK CHILI POWDER

½ TEASPOON CHIPOTLE POWDER

½ TEASPOON BLACK PEPPER

½ TEASPOON ONION POWDER

½ TEASPOON GARLIC POWDER

¼ TEASPOON PAPRIKA

½ TABLESPOON KOSHER SALT

Chili-Dusted Cauliflower & Chickpea Salad

YIELD: **4 TO 6 SERVINGS**

ACTIVE TIME: **25 MINUTES**

TOTAL TIME: **45 MINUTES**

Crunchy cauliflower, nutty chickpeas, and a perfect balance of sweet and spicy place this salad a cut above its peers.

DIRECTIONS

1. Preheat the oven to 400°F. To prepare the salad, place all of the ingredients in a mixing bowl and toss until the cauliflower and chickpeas are evenly coated. Place the mixture in a 9 x 13-inch baking pan, place the pan in the oven, and roast until the cauliflower is slightly charred and still crunchy, about 30 minutes. Remove from the oven and let the mixture cool slightly.

2. To prepare the dressing, place all of the ingredients in a large mixing bowl and stir until the sugar has dissolved. Place the cooked cauliflower-and-chickpea mixture in the bowl, toss to coat, and serve.

Coconut & Cucumber Salad

YIELD: **4 SERVINGS**

ACTIVE TIME: **10 MINUTES**

TOTAL TIME: **25 MINUTES**

The combination of warming, pungent cumin, sweet and soothing coconut, and crispy cucumber is endlessly satisfying.

INGREDIENTS

5 LARGE CUCUMBERS, PEELED, HALVED LENGTHWISE, AND SEEDED

½ CUP SHREDDED UNSWEETENED COCONUT

ZEST AND JUICE OF 2 LIMES

¼ CUP COCONUT MILK

1 TEASPOON CHILI GARLIC SAUCE, PLUS MORE AS NEEDED

½-INCH PIECE FRESH GINGER, PEELED AND GRATED

1 TEASPOON SUGAR

1 TEASPOON CUMIN

1 TEASPOON KOSHER SALT, PLUS MORE TO TASTE

6 SCALLIONS, TRIMMED AND SLICED THIN, FOR SERVING

½ CUP ROASTED PEANUTS, CHOPPED, FOR SERVING

DIRECTIONS

1. Quarter each cucumber half and then cut the quarters into long, ⅛-inch-wide strips. Place the strips on paper towels to drain for 15 minutes.

2. Place the coconut, lime juice, coconut milk, chili garlic sauce, ginger, sugar, cumin, and salt in a small food processor or a blender and puree until smooth.

3. Place the cucumbers in a large serving bowl. Top with the coconut mixture and toss to coat.

4. Sprinkle the lime zest, scallions, and peanuts on top of the dressed noodles, season to taste, and serve immediately.

YIELD: **4 SERVINGS**

ACTIVE TIME: **20 MINUTES**

TOTAL TIME: **20 MINUTES**

Rice Bowl with Benihana's Ginger Dressing

The restaurant chain's famed dressing lifts what should be a humble bowl of rice and vegetables.

INGREDIENTS

FOR THE RICE BOWL

1 TABLESPOON OLIVE OIL

1 LB. EXTRA-FIRM TOFU, DRAINED AND CHOPPED

2 CUPS COOKED WHITE RICE, AT ROOM TEMPERATURE

2 CARROTS, PEELED AND GRATED

1 CUP BROCCOLI SPROUTS

1 CUP CORN KERNELS

1 CUP EDAMAME

FLESH FROM 2 AVOCADOS, SLICED

SALT, TO TASTE

SESAME SEEDS, FOR GARNISH

FOR THE DRESSING

¼ CUP CHOPPED WHITE ONION

¼ CUP PEANUT OIL

1 TABLESPOON RICE VINEGAR

1-INCH PIECE FRESH GINGER, PEELED AND MINCED

1 TABLESPOON MINCED CELERY

1 TABLESPOON SOY SAUCE

1 TEASPOON TOMATO PASTE

1½ TEASPOONS SUGAR

1 TEASPOON FRESH LEMON JUICE

½ TEASPOON KOSHER SALT

BLACK PEPPER, TO TASTE

DIRECTIONS

1. To begin preparations for the rice bowl, place the oil in a large skillet and warm over medium-high heat. When the oil starts to shimmer, add the tofu and cook until it is browned all over, turning the pieces as necessary.

2. To prepare the dressing, place all of the ingredients in a blender or food processor and puree until smooth.

3. Divide the rice between four bowls. Arrange the tofu, carrots, broccoli sprouts, corn, edamame, and avocados on top of each portion.

4. Top each portion with a pinch of salt and the dressing, garnish with the sesame seeds, and serve.

Fennel, Grapefruit & Pistachio Salad

YIELD: **2 SERVINGS**

ACTIVE TIME: **10 MINUTES**

TOTAL TIME: **10 MINUTES**

While this may seem like an odd combination, the individual flavors come together better than you'd ever expect.

INGREDIENTS

1 RUBY RED GRAPEFRUIT

½ LARGE FENNEL BULB, TRIMMED, CORED, AND SLICED VERY THIN

1 TABLESPOON OLIVE OIL

¼ TEASPOON KOSHER SALT

BLACK PEPPER, TO TASTE

2 TABLESPOONS SHELLED AND CHOPPED PISTACHIOS

DIRECTIONS

1. Trim the top and bottom from the grapefruit and place it cut-side up. Cut along the contour of the fruit to remove the pith and peel. Cut one segment, lengthwise, between the pulp and the membrane. Make a similar slice on the other side of the segment and then remove the pulp. Set aside and repeat with the remaining segments. This technique is known as "supreming," and can be used for all citrus fruits. When all of the pulp has been removed from the segments, chop it and place it in a salad bowl.

2. Place the fennel in the bowl, drizzle with olive oil, season with the salt and pepper, and add the pistachios. Stir until combined and serve.

Cold Green Bean Salad

YIELD: **4 SERVINGS**

ACTIVE TIME: **10 MINUTES**

TOTAL TIME: **15 MINUTES**

A good time to use a high-quality blue cheese such as Stilton, Roquefort, or the famed Bayley Hazen Blue from Vermont's famed Jasper Hill Farm.

INGREDIENTS

1 LB. GREEN BEANS, TRIMMED

SALT, TO TASTE

1 TEASPOON DIJON MUSTARD

1½ TEASPOONS MINCED SHALLOT

2 TABLESPOONS WHITE WINE VINEGAR

⅓ CUP OLIVE OIL

BLACK PEPPER, TO TASTE

½ CUP CRUMBLED BLUE CHEESE

½ CUP CHOPPED WALNUTS

DIRECTIONS

1. Bring water to a boil in a large saucepan. Once water is boiling, add the beans and salt and cook until al dente, about 5 minutes.

2. Drain and run the beans under cold water to stop the cooking process. Pat dry with a towel.

3. Whisk together the mustard, shallot, vinegar, and olive oil and set aside. Place the blue cheese, walnuts, and the green beans in a salad bowl. Add the vinaigrette, toss to combine, and serve cold or at room temperature.

Tabbouleh with Feta

YIELD: **4 CUPS**

ACTIVE TIME: **10 MINUTES**

TOTAL TIME: **40 MINUTES**

This recipe includes traditional ingredients like tomato and cucumber but feel free to add any raw vegetable you like. Look for bulgur wheat in the bulk aisle, as it is less expensive there than in the prepackaged blends.

INGREDIENTS

½ CUP BULGUR WHEAT

1 ½ CUPS BOILING WATER

½ TEASPOON KOSHER SALT, PLUS MORE TO TASTE

½ CUP FRESH LEMON JUICE

2 CUPS FRESH FLAT-LEAF PARSLEY, CHOPPED

1 CUP PEELED, SEEDED, AND DICED CUCUMBER

1 TOMATO, DICED

¼ CUP SLICED SCALLIONS

1 CUP FRESH MINT LEAVES, CHOPPED

2 TABLESPOONS OLIVE OIL

BLACK PEPPER, TO TASTE

MESCLUN SALAD GREENS, FOR SERVING

½ CUP CRUMBLED FETA CHEESE, FOR GARNISH

DIRECTIONS

1. Place the bulgur in a heatproof bowl and add the boiling water, salt, and half of the lemon juice. Cover and let sit for about 20 minutes or until the bulgur has absorbed the water and is tender. Drain any excess water if necessary. Let the bulgur cool completely.

2. When the bulgur is completely cooled, add the parsley, cucumber, tomato, scallions, mint, olive oil, black pepper, and remaining lemon juice. Taste and add more salt if necessary.

3. When ready to serve, place on a plate with the salad greens and top with the feta and some of the remaining lemon juice.

Noodle Salad with Nuoc Cham

YIELD: **4 SERVINGS**

ACTIVE TIME: **30 MINUTES**

TOTAL TIME: **1 HOUR**

A cold noodle salad is just the thing on a hot day. Assemble this tangy dish the next time the reading on the thermometer starts to climb.

INGREDIENTS

FOR THE SALAD

1 LB. EXTRA-FIRM TOFU

2 CUPS MUNG BEAN SPROUTS

½ LB. RICE STICK NOODLES

¼ CUP PEANUT OIL

SALT, TO TASTE

1 RED BELL PEPPER, STEMMED, SEEDED, AND JULIENNED

2½ CUPS GRATED ROMAINE LETTUCE

2 HANDFULS MIXED FRESH HERB LEAVES, CHOPPED OR TORN (MINT, CILANTRO, BASIL)

2 SMALL CUCUMBERS, PEELED AND JULIENNED

2 TABLESPOONS CHOPPED PEANUTS, FOR GARNISH

FOR THE NUOC CHAM

⅓ CUP HOT WATER (125°F)

¼ CUP FRESH LIME JUICE

Continued...

DIRECTIONS

1. To begin preparations for the salad, drain and cut the tofu into ½-inch strips. Arrange them in a single layer on a paper towel–lined tray. Cover with paper towels and pat dry. Let sit for 30 minutes, changing the paper towels halfway through. Cut the dried strips into ½-inch cubes and set aside.

2. Bring a large pot of water to a boil. As it heats up, pick over the bean sprouts, discarding any discolored or spoiled ones. Put the remaining sprouts in a bowl of cold water. Discard the hulls that float to the top, then rinse the remaining sprouts under cold water. Add the sprouts to the boiling water and cook for 1 minute. Remove with a strainer and immediately run under cold water to stop them from cooking further. Drain well and chop.

3. Add the noodles to the pot of boiling water and stir for the first minute to prevent any sticking. Cook until they are tender but chewy, 5 to 7 minutes. Drain, rinse under cold water, and drain again.

4. Heat a large, deep skillet over medium heat for 2 to 3 minutes. Add the oil, raise heat to medium-high, and let warm for about 2 minutes. As the oil heats up, gently blot the tofu pieces with paper towels one more time to absorb as much surface moisture as possible and sprinkle with salt. When the oil begins to shimmer, add the tofu to the skillet in a

Continued...

¼ CUP SOY SAUCE

¼ CUP BROWN SUGAR

3 TABLESPOONS RICE VINEGAR

3 GARLIC CLOVES, MINCED

1-INCH PIECE FRESH GINGER, PEELED AND GRATED

1 HOT CHILI PEPPER (SUCH AS FRESNO OR JALAPEÑO), SEEDED AND CHOPPED

single layer, working in batches if necessary. Make sure there is plenty of room in the skillet, as the tofu pieces will cook better. Cook until golden on all sides, 4 to 6 minutes total. Transfer to a paper towel–lined plate to absorb the oil.

5. To prepare the nuoc cham, place all of the ingredients in a small bowl and stir until the sugar has dissolved.

6. Divide the noodles among four shallow bowls. Arrange the lettuce, herbs, cucumber, and tofu on top. Top with the nuoc cham, garnish with the peanuts, and serve.

CHAPTER 4

SOUPS

Universally identified with comfort. Able to be prepared with ease. Accepting of an incredible amount of flavors. There are dishes that might be more impressive than soups, but none that are more beloved.

Containing a balance of low-and-slow favorites and ready-in-a-flash preparations, the majority of the soups in this section will make for a perfect light lunch or first course, but some are hearty enough to serve as the main event. Whichever one you choose, you can be sure it will soothe your mind and body, no matter what shape your day has taken.

Vegan Tom Yam Gung with Tofu

YIELD: **4 SERVINGS**

ACTIVE TIME: **20 MINUTES**

TOTAL TIME: **45 MINUTES**

This hot-and-sour soup traditionally contains shrimp, but is so fragrant that this vegan twist feels like it wants for nothing.

INGREDIENTS

¼ CUP OLIVE OIL

1 ONION, MINCED

1 GARLIC CLOVE, MINCED

6 CUPS VEGETABLE STOCK (SEE PAGE 12)

¼ CUP FRESH LIME JUICE

3 MAKRUT LIME LEAVES

3 BIRD'S EYE CHILI PEPPERS, STEMMED, SEEDED, AND SLICED

2 TABLESPOONS FINELY CHOPPED FRESH CILANTRO

1 LEMONGRASS STALK, BRUISED

1 TABLESPOON SUGAR

¾ LB. EXTRA-FIRM TOFU, DRAINED AND CHOPPED

¼ CUP SOY SAUCE

8 SHIITAKE MUSHROOMS, SLICED

SALT AND PEPPER, TO TASTE

WATERCRESS, FOR GARNISH

BEAN SPROUTS, FOR GARNISH

DIRECTIONS

1. In a medium saucepan, add 2 tablespoons of the oil and warm over medium heat. When the oil starts to shimmer, add the onion and garlic and cook, stirring frequently, until the onion softens, about 5 minutes. Add the stock, lime juice, lime leaves, chilies, cilantro, lemongrass stalk, and sugar and bring to a boil.

2. Meanwhile, in a large sauté pan, add the remaining oil and warm over medium heat. Add the tofu and cook, stirring frequently, until lightly browned on all sides. Remove from the pan and set aside.

3. Strain the broth through a fine sieve, discard the solids, and place the liquid in a clean pan. Add the soy sauce and shiitake mushrooms and bring to a simmer. Add the tofu and cook for 4 additional minutes.

4. Season with salt and pepper, ladle into warmed bowls, and garnish with the watercress and bean sprouts.

INGREDIENTS

1 CUP BROWN LENTILS

½ CUP FRENCH LENTILS

4 CUPS VEGETABLE STOCK (SEE PAGE 12)

3 CARROTS, WASHED AND CHOPPED

1 LARGE WHITE ONION, PEELED AND CHOPPED

3 GARLIC CLOVES, MINCED

3-INCH PIECE FRESH GINGER, PEELED AND MINCED

ZEST AND JUICE OF 1 LEMON

3 TABLESPOONS SMOKED PAPRIKA

2 TABLESPOONS CINNAMON

1 TABLESPOON GROUND CORIANDER

1 TABLESPOON TURMERIC

1 TABLESPOON CUMIN

1½ TEASPOONS ALLSPICE

2 TO 3 BAY LEAVES

SALT AND PEPPER, TO TASTE

1 (14 OZ.) CAN CANNELLINI BEANS

FRESH MINT, FINELY CHOPPED, FOR GARNISH

GOAT CHEESE, CRUMBLED, FOR GARNISH

Moroccan Lentil Stew

Set this incredibly filling stew on before you head out the door in the morning and you'll have a delicious dinner waiting for you when you come home.

DIRECTIONS

1. Place the lentils in a fine sieve and rinse to remove any impurities. Place all of the ingredients, save the cannellini beans and the garnishes, in a slow cooker. Cover and cook on low for 7½ hours.

2. After 7½ hours, add the cannellini beans. Stir, cover, and cook for 30 minutes. Ladle into warmed bowls and garnish with the mint and goat cheese.

Roasted Corn & Red Pepper Soup

YIELD: **4 SERVINGS**

ACTIVE TIME: **30 MINUTES**

TOTAL TIME: **1 HOUR AND 30 MINUTES**

The bit of char that comes from roasting the corn and peppers tempers their natural sweetness just enough.

INGREDIENTS

3 CUPS FRESH CORN KERNELS

2 TABLESPOONS OLIVE OIL

SALT AND PEPPER, TO TASTE

3 RED PEPPERS

4 TABLESPOONS UNSALTED BUTTER

½ CUP HEAVY CREAM

½ CUP MILK

SOUR CREAM, FOR GARNISH

DIRECTIONS

1. Preheat the oven to 375°F. Place the corn in a single layer on a large baking sheet and drizzle with the oil. Season with salt, place in the oven, and roast until the corn starts to darken and caramelize, 12 to 18 minutes. Remove from the oven and raise the temperature to 425°F.

2. Place the peppers on another baking sheet and place them in the oven. Cook, while turning occasionally, until the skins are blistered all over, about 30 minutes. Remove from the oven and let cool. When cool enough to handle, remove the skins and seeds and discard. Set the peppers aside.

3. Place the corn, peppers, butter, cream, and milk in a saucepan and bring to a simmer over medium heat while stirring. Simmer for 20 minutes, making sure that the soup does not come to a boil. After simmering for 20 minutes, remove the soup from heat and let cool for 10 minutes.

4. Transfer the soup to a blender and puree until smooth. If the soup has cooled too much, return it to the saucepan and cook until warmed through. When ready, ladle into warmed bowls, garnish with sour cream, and serve.

Pumpkin Bisque with Spiced Crème Fraîche

YIELD: **6 SERVINGS**

ACTIVE TIME: **25 MINUTES**

TOTAL TIME: **2 HOURS**

The Long Island Cheese pumpkin's meaty, dense flesh and sweet, earthy flavor makes it ideal for this modern-leaning bisque.

INGREDIENTS

FOR THE BISQUE

1 LONG ISLAND CHEESE PUMPKIN

6 TABLESPOONS UNSALTED BUTTER

2 YELLOW ONIONS, SLICED

3 GARLIC CLOVES, MINCED

4 CUPS MILK

1 CUP HEAVY CREAM

2 TABLESPOONS BROWN SUGAR

1 TABLESPOON KOSHER SALT, PLUS ½ TEASPOON

1 TABLESPOON OLIVE OIL

¼ TEASPOON BLACK PEPPER

¼ TEASPOON PAPRIKA

MAPLE SYRUP, FOR GARNISH

FOR THE CRÈME FRAÎCHE

1 CUP CRÈME FRAÎCHE (SEE PAGE 190 FOR HOMEMADE)

½ TEASPOON CINNAMON

⅛ TEASPOON GROUND NUTMEG

⅛ TEASPOON GROUND CLOVES

1 TABLESPOON MAPLE SYRUP

DIRECTIONS

1. To begin preparations for the bisque, preheat the oven to 350°F. Cut the pumpkin in half lengthwise, remove the seeds, and reserve them. Place the halves of pumpkin cut-side down on an aluminum foil–lined baking sheet. Place the pumpkin in the oven and roast until the flesh is tender, about 40 minutes. Remove from the oven, taking care not to spill any of the juices, and let cool. Leave the oven on.

2. Place the butter in a saucepan and melt over medium-high heat. Add the onions and garlic and cook until the onions are translucent, about 3 minutes.

3. Add the milk, cream, sugar, and tablespoon of salt and reduce the heat to medium. Scrape the flesh from the pumpkin into the pan. Bring the soup to a boil and then reduce the heat so that it simmers. Cook, while stirring occasionally, for 20 minutes.

4. While the soup is simmering, run the reserved pumpkin seeds under water to remove any pulp. Pat them dry, place them on a baking sheet, drizzle with the olive oil, and sprinkle them with the remaining salt, the pepper, and paprika. Place in the oven and bake until light brown and crispy, 6 to 8 minutes. Remove from the oven and set aside.

5. To prepare the crème fraîche, place all of the ingredients in a bowl, stir to combine, and set aside.

6. Working in batches, place the soup in a blender and puree until smooth. Season to taste, ladle into bowls, and top each portion with a dollop of the spiced crème fraîche, the toasted pumpkin seeds, and a drizzle of maple syrup.

Creamy Curry Kuri Soup

YIELD: **6 SERVINGS**

ACTIVE TIME: **30 MINUTES**

TOTAL TIME: **2 HOURS**

Kuri is a thin-skinned, orange squash with a flavor similar to chestnuts. It sounds exotic, but you can likely find it at your local farmers market.

INGREDIENTS

1 LARGE KURI SQUASH, QUARTERED

1 LARGE ONION, SLICED

2 TABLESPOONS OLIVE OIL

SALT AND PEPPER, TO TASTE

2 TABLESPOONS CURRY POWDER

4 TABLESPOONS UNSALTED BUTTER

1 CUP HEAVY CREAM

1 CUP WHOLE MILK

2 SPRIGS FRESH ROSEMARY

2 SPRIGS FRESH THYME

DIRECTIONS

1. Preheat the oven to 400°F. Place the squash and onion in a baking dish, drizzle with the oil, and season with salt. Place the dish in the oven and roast until the onion has browned, 15 to 25 minutes. Remove the dish from the oven, transfer the onion to a bowl, return the squash to the oven and roast until the flesh is tender, another 20 to 35 minutes. Remove the squash from the oven and let cool.

2. When the squash is cool enough to handle, scoop out the seeds. Scrape the flesh into the bowl containing the onion.

3. Place the squash, onion, and remaining ingredients in a large saucepan and bring to a boil over medium-high heat. Reduce heat to low and let the mixture simmer, while stirring occasionally, for 15 to 20 minutes.

4. Remove the thyme and rosemary sprigs and discard. Transfer the soup to a blender and puree until desired texture is achieved. Season with salt and pepper and ladle into warmed bowls.

NOTE: The toasted squash seeds will make for a lovely garnish for this soup. To utilize them in this manner, wash the seeds to remove any pulp and then pat them dry. Transfer them to a baking sheet, drizzle with olive oil, sprinkle with salt, and place the sheet in the oven. Bake for 5 minutes, remove them from the oven, and turn them over. Return to the oven and bake for another 5 minutes, until golden brown.

Artichoke Soup with Fennel Seed Yogurt

YIELD: **4 SERVINGS**

ACTIVE TIME: **20 MINUTES**

TOTAL TIME: **40 MINUTES**

Artichokes are a vegetable that people tend to shy away from, making them perfect for the comforting cloak a soup can provide.

INGREDIENTS

FOR THE SOUP

6 ARTICHOKES

1 TABLESPOON OLIVE OIL

1 TABLESPOON UNSALTED BUTTER

1 GARLIC CLOVE, MINCED

1 YELLOW ONION, CHOPPED

1 CUP RIESLING

LEAVES FROM 1 SPRIG FRESH THYME, CHOPPED

4 CUPS HEAVY CREAM

1 CUP VEGETABLE STOCK (SEE PAGE 12)

SALT AND PEPPER, TO TASTE

FRESH DILL, FINELY CHOPPED, FOR GARNISH

FOR THE YOGURT

1 CUP PLAIN GREEK YOGURT

2 TABLESPOONS PERNOD

1 TEASPOON GROUND FENNEL

DIRECTIONS

1. To begin preparations for the soup, peel the artichokes, remove the hearts, and slice them thin.

2. Place the oil and butter in a medium saucepan. Add the artichoke hearts, garlic, and onion and cook over medium heat for 10 minutes.

3. Add the Riesling and thyme and cook until the wine has reduced by half. Add the heavy cream and the stock and simmer for 10 minutes.

4. While the soup is simmering, prepare the yogurt. Place all of the ingredients in a mixing bowl, stir to combine, and refrigerate until ready to use.

5. Transfer the soup to a food processor or blender, puree until smooth, and strain through a fine sieve. Season with salt and pepper, ladle into warmed bowls, serve with the fennel seed yogurt, and garnish with dill.

Carrot & Ginger Soup with Turmeric Cream

YIELD: **4 SERVINGS**

ACTIVE TIME: **25 MINUTES**

TOTAL TIME: **1 HOUR**

It turns out that earthy turmeric and spicy ginger are precisely what the sweetness of carrots cries out for.

INGREDIENTS

4 TABLESPOONS UNSALTED BUTTER

2 YELLOW ONIONS, DICED

6 CARROTS, PEELED AND CHOPPED

4-INCH PIECE FRESH GINGER, PEELED AND MINCED

ZEST AND JUICE OF 2 ORANGES

1 CUP WHITE WINE

8 CUPS VEGETABLE STOCK (SEE PAGE 12), PLUS MORE AS NEEDED

SALT AND PEPPER, TO TASTE

FRESH DILL, FINELY CHOPPED, FOR GARNISH

FOR THE TURMERIC CREAM

½ CUP HEAVY CREAM

½ TEASPOON TURMERIC

1 PINCH KOSHER SALT

DIRECTIONS

1. To begin preparations for the soup, place the butter in a medium saucepan and melt over medium heat. Add the onions and cook until they start to soften, about 5 minutes.

2. Add the carrots, ginger, and orange zest. Cook for 5 minutes, or until the carrots start to soften. Add the orange juice and white wine and cook until evaporated. Add the stock, bring to a boil, and season with salt and pepper. Reduce heat so that the soup simmers and cook for 10 to 15 minutes, until the vegetables are tender.

3. Transfer the soup to a food processor or blender, puree until smooth, and strain through a fine sieve. Return the soup to a clean saucepan and adjust the seasoning. Add more stock if the consistency is too thick. Bring the soup back to a gentle simmer and then remove from heat.

4. To prepare the turmeric cream, place the cream in a bowl and beat it at high speed using a handheld mixer fitted with the whisk attachment until soft peaks start to form. Add the turmeric and salt and stir to incorporate.

5. Ladle the soup into warm bowls, top each portion with a dollop of the turmeric cream, and garnish with the dill.

YIELD: **6 SERVINGS**

ACTIVE TIME: **30 MINUTES**

TOTAL TIME: **45 MINUTES**

Irish Leek Soup with Blue Cheese Fritters

The robust flavor and golden color of Ireland's famed Cashel Blue cheese let this soup linger in the memory long after the meal is over.

INGREDIENTS

FOR THE SOUP

4 TABLESPOONS UNSALTED BUTTER

2 TABLESPOONS OLIVE OIL

3 LARGE LEEKS, TRIMMED, RINSED WELL, AND SLICED THIN

½ LB. CASHEL BLUE CHEESE

2 TABLESPOONS ALL-PURPOSE FLOUR

1 TABLESPOON WHOLE-GRAIN MUSTARD, PLUS MORE FOR GARNISH

6 CUPS VEGETABLE STOCK (SEE PAGE 12)

BLACK PEPPER, TO TASTE

FRESH CHIVES, FINELY CHOPPED, FOR GARNISH

FOR THE FRITTERS

4 CUPS VEGETABLE OIL

6 OZ. CASHEL BLUE CHEESE

3 EGGS

¼ CUP ALL-PURPOSE FLOUR

1 CUP PANKO BREAD CRUMBS, FINELY GROUND

DIRECTIONS

1. To begin preparations for the soup, place the butter and oil in a large saucepan and warm over low heat. Add the leeks and cook until they start to soften, about 5 minutes.

2. Break the Cashel blue cheese into small pieces and add to the saucepan. Cook, while stirring, until the cheese is melted. Add the flour and cook for 2 minutes, while stirring constantly, then incorporate the mustard.

3. Slowly add the stock, stirring to prevent any lumps from forming. Bring to a boil, reduce heat so that the soup simmers, and cook for 10 minutes.

4. While the soup is simmering, prepare the fritters. Place the oil in a medium saucepan and heat to 350°F. Cut the blue cheese into 12 cubes. Place the eggs in a bowl and beat with a fork. Place the flour and bread crumbs in separate bowls. Dredge the cheese in the flour and shake to remove any excess. Dredge the cheese in the egg wash until evenly coated. Remove from the egg wash, shake to remove any excess, and dredge in the bread crumbs until coated. Place the coated cheese in the hot oil and fry until golden brown. Use a slotted spoon to remove the fritters from the oil, set on paper towels to drain, and season with salt.

5. Season the soup with pepper and ladle into warm bowls. Garnish with chives and additional mustard and serve with the blue cheese fritters.

White Tomato Soup with Confit Cherry Tomatoes

It is very important to choose ripe tomatoes for this dish. If they are even slightly off, this soup can get overly acidic.

YIELD: **4 SERVINGS**

ACTIVE TIME: **45 MINUTES**

TOTAL TIME: **24 HOURS**

INGREDIENTS

FOR THE SOUP

10 LARGE RIPE TOMATOES, CHOPPED

LEAVES FROM 1 SPRIG FRESH THYME, CHOPPED

1 STAR ANISE POD

1 TABLESPOON JASMINE RICE

2 CUPS HEAVY CREAM

SALT AND PEPPER, TO TASTE

FOR THE CONFIT CHERRY TOMATOES

12 CHERRY TOMATOES

1 GARLIC CLOVE, SLICED VERY THIN

ZEST OF 1 LEMON

1 TABLESPOON OLIVE OIL

SALT AND PEPPER, TO TASTE

DIRECTIONS

1. To begin preparations for the soup, place the tomatoes in a food processor and puree for 5 minutes. Working over a large bowl, strain the puree through cheesecloth overnight.

2. Place the strained tomato water, thyme, star anise pod, and rice in a medium saucepan and cook over medium heat until the liquid has reduced by half. Add the cream and gently simmer for 30 minutes.

3. While the soup is simmering, preheat the oven to 300°F and prepare the confit cherry tomatoes. Place the tomatoes on a baking sheet and sprinkle the garlic and lemon zest over them. Drizzle with olive oil and season with salt and pepper. Place in oven and roast for 15 minutes, until the tomatoes' skins are blistered and they start to collapse. Remove from the oven and let cool.

4. Remove the star anise pod from the soup and discard. Transfer the soup to a food processor and puree until smooth and creamy. Strain through a fine sieve, return to the pan, season with salt and pepper, and bring to a simmer.

5. Ladle the soup into bowls and serve with the confit cherry tomatoes.

Iranian Barley Soup

YIELD: **4 SERVINGS**

ACTIVE TIME: **20 MINUTES**

TOTAL TIME: **1 HOUR AND 30 MINUTES**

Here is a thick, delicious soup that gets its beautiful color from tomato paste and turmeric.

INGREDIENTS

2 TABLESPOONS OLIVE OIL

2 ONIONS, CHOPPED

2 CARROTS, PEELED AND CHOPPED

1 CUP PEARL BARLEY

3 TABLESPOONS TOMATO PASTE

1 TEASPOON TURMERIC

8 CUPS VEGETABLE STOCK (SEE PAGE 12)

½ CUP SOUR CREAM

⅓ CUP FINELY CHOPPED FRESH PARSLEY LEAVES

SALT AND PEPPER, TO TASTE

8 LIME WEDGES, FOR SERVING

DIRECTIONS

1. Place the oil in a large saucepan and warm over medium heat. When the oil starts to shimmer, add the onions and cook until they start to soften, about 5 minutes. Add the carrots, barley, tomato paste, and turmeric and cook for 2 minutes.

2. Add the stock and bring the soup to a boil. Reduce heat so that the soup simmers and cook until the barley is tender, about 1 hour.

3. Remove the soup from heat. Add the sour cream and parsley and season with salt and pepper. Ladle into warmed bowls and serve with the lime wedges.

African Peanut & Quinoa Soup

YIELD: 4 SERVINGS

ACTIVE TIME: 20 MINUTES

TOTAL TIME: 45 MINUTES

The quinoa lends a bit of body and even more nuttiness to a traditional African peanut soup.

INGREDIENTS

1 TABLESPOON OLIVE OIL

1 TABLESPOON UNSALTED BUTTER

1 RED ONION, CHOPPED

1 CUP CHOPPED SWEET POTATO

1 GREEN BELL PEPPER, STEMMED, SEEDED, AND CHOPPED

2 CELERY STALKS, CHOPPED

1 ZUCCHINI, CHOPPED

1 JALAPEÑO PEPPER, STEMMED, SEEDED, AND MINCED

1 GARLIC CLOVE, MINCED

6 CUPS VEGETABLE STOCK (SEE PAGE 12)

¾ CUP QUINOA

1 TEASPOON CUMIN

½ CUP PEANUT BUTTER

SALT AND PEPPER, TO TASTE

FRESH OREGANO, FINELY CHOPPED, FOR GARNISH

PEANUTS, TOASTED, FOR GARNISH

DIRECTIONS

1. Place the oil and butter in a large saucepan and warm over medium heat. When the butter has melted, add the red onion, sweet potato, bell pepper, celery, zucchini, jalapeño, and garlic and cook until the vegetables are soft, about 10 minutes.

2. Add the stock and bring to a boil. Reduce heat so that the soup simmers, add the quinoa and cumin, cover, and simmer until quinoa is tender, about 15 minutes.

3. Stir in the peanut butter and season with salt and pepper. Ladle into warm bowls garnish with the oregano and toasted peanuts.

Spring Pea Soup with Lemon Ricotta

YIELD: **4 SERVINGS**

ACTIVE TIME: **15 MINUTES**

TOTAL TIME: **25 MINUTES**

Early in the spring, peas are absolutely perfect—tender enough that they don't require a long cook time and bursting with country-fresh flavor. Pair them with creamy, zesty lemon ricotta and you've got a dish that positively sings.

INGREDIENTS

1 CUP RICOTTA CHEESE

¼ CUP HEAVY CREAM

2 TABLESPOONS LEMON ZEST

1 TABLESPOON KOSHER SALT, PLUS 2 TEASPOONS

12 CUPS WATER

6 STRIPS LEMON PEEL

3 CUPS PEAS

3 SHALLOTS, DICED

6 FRESH MINT LEAVES, PLUS MORE FOR GARNISH

DIRECTIONS

1. Place the ricotta, cream, lemon zest, and the 2 teaspoons of salt in a food processor and puree until smooth. Season to taste and set aside.

2. Place the water and remaining salt in a saucepan and bring to a boil over medium heat. Add the strips of lemon peel to the saucepan along with the peas and shallots. Cook for 2 to 3 minutes, until the peas are just cooked through. Drain, making sure to reserve 2 cups of the cooking liquid, and immediately transfer the peas, strips of lemon peel, and shallots to a blender. Add the mint leaves and half of the reserved cooking liquid, and puree until the desired consistency is achieved, adding more cooking liquid as needed.

3. Season to taste, ladle into warmed bowls, and place a spoonful of the lemon ricotta in each bowl. Garnish with additional mint and serve immediately, as the brilliant green color starts to fade as the soup cools.

Heirloom Tomato & Smoked Cheddar Soup

YIELD: **6 SERVINGS**

ACTIVE TIME: **20 MINUTES**

TOTAL TIME: **1 HOUR AND 15 MINUTES**

The end of tomato season is always bittersweet, as it also signals the end of summer. This creamy soup is one of the easiest ways to handle the transition to the crisp, cool air of fall.

INGREDIENTS

2 STICKS UNSALTED BUTTER

1 SMALL RED ONION, SLICED

3 CELERY STALKS, SLICED

10 GARLIC CLOVES, SLICED

1 TABLESPOON KOSHER SALT, PLUS MORE TO TASTE

½ CUP ALL-PURPOSE FLOUR

8 HEIRLOOM TOMATOES, CHOPPED

3 CUPS MARINARA SAUCE (SEE PAGE 27)

1 TABLESPOON TOMATO PASTE

4 CUPS VEGETABLE STOCK (SEE PAGE 12)

1 PARMESAN CHEESE RIND (OPTIONAL)

1 CUP HEAVY CREAM

1 CUP GRATED SMOKED CHEDDAR CHEESE

10 FRESH BASIL LEAVES, SLICED THIN

BLACK PEPPER, TO TASTE

DIRECTIONS

1. Place the butter in a large saucepan and melt over medium heat. Add the onion, celery, garlic, and salt and cook until the onion is translucent, about 3 minutes.

2. Add the flour and cook until it gives off a nutty aroma, stirring constantly to ensure that it does not brown too quickly. Add the tomatoes, Marinara Sauce, tomato paste, stock, and, if using, the Parmesan rind. Stir to incorporate and let the soup come to a boil. Reduce heat so that the soup simmers and cook for 30 minutes. Taste to see if the flavor is to your liking. If not, continue to simmer until it is.

3. Stir the cream, cheddar, and basil into the soup. If you used the Parmesan rind, remove it, transfer the soup to a blender, and puree until smooth. Season with salt and pepper and ladle into warmed bowls.

Raspberry & Tomato Gazpacho

YIELD: **4 TO 6 SERVINGS**

ACTIVE TIME: **10 MINUTES**

TOTAL TIME: **24 HOURS**

Roasting the tomatoes adds considerable depth to this dish, which would otherwise be overwhelmed by the sweet-and-tart flavor of the raspberries.

INGREDIENTS

2 TO 3 LARGE HEIRLOOM TOMATOES

1 CUP RASPBERRIES

2 GARLIC CLOVES

½ CUP PEELED AND DICED CUCUMBER

2 TEASPOONS FRESH LEMON JUICE

2 TABLESPOONS OLIVE OIL

1 RED BELL PEPPER, STEMMED, SEEDED, AND CHOPPED

SALT AND PEPPER, TO TASTE

FRESH MINT LEAVES, FOR GARNISH

HEAVY CREAM, FOR GARNISH (OPTIONAL)

DIRECTIONS

1. Preheat the oven to 425°F. Place the tomatoes on a baking sheet and roast until they start to collapse and their skins start to blister, about 10 to 15 minutes. Remove from the oven and let cool slightly.

2. Place the tomatoes and all of the remaining ingredients, except for the garnishes, in a blender, puree until smooth, and refrigerate overnight.

3. When ready to serve, ladle the soup into bowls and garnish each portion with mint leaves and, if desired, approximately 1 tablespoon of heavy cream.

Broken Pasta Soup

YIELD: **4 SERVINGS**

ACTIVE TIME: **20 MINUTES**

TOTAL TIME: **45 MINUTES**

A lovely dish for those nights when you don't have time to go to the store and a simple bowl of pasta won't quite do.

INGREDIENTS

1 TABLESPOON OLIVE OIL

1 ONION, CHOPPED

2 GARLIC CLOVES, MINCED

2 CARROTS, PEELED AND CHOPPED

1 ZUCCHINI, CHOPPED

4 CELERY STALKS, CHOPPED

1 (28 OZ.) CAN STEWED TOMATOES

4 CUPS VEGETABLE STOCK (SEE PAGE 12)

1 CUP BROKEN SPAGHETTI (½-INCH PIECES)

2 TABLESPOONS FINELY CHOPPED FRESH PARSLEY

SALT AND PEPPER, TO TASTE

BASIL PESTO (SEE PAGE 24), FOR SERVING

DIRECTIONS

1. Place the oil in a large saucepan and warm over medium heat. When the oil starts to shimmer, add the onion and cook until it starts to soften, about 5 minutes.

2. Add the garlic, carrots, zucchini, and celery and cook for 5 minutes. Add the tomatoes and stock and bring to a boil. Reduce heat so that the soup simmers and cook for 15 minutes.

3. Add the spaghetti and cook until it is tender, 6 to 8 minutes.

4. Stir in the parsley and season with salt and pepper. Ladle into warmed bowls and serve alongside the pesto.

Curried Carrot Soup

YIELD: **4 SERVINGS**

ACTIVE TIME: **20 MINUTES**

TOTAL TIME: **45 MINUTES**

Jaggery, an unrefined sugar that is popular in numerous Asian cuisines, beautifully tempers the spice in this soup. If you cannot find it at the store, brown sugar will work.

INGREDIENTS

1 TABLESPOON OLIVE OIL

1 ONION, CHOPPED

1 GARLIC CLOVE, MINCED

2 TABLESPOONS CURRY POWDER

6 CUPS VEGETABLE STOCK (SEE PAGE 12)

1 BIRD'S EYE CHILI PEPPER, STEMMED, SEEDED, AND SLICED

ZEST AND JUICE OF 1 LIME

2 TABLESPOONS SOY SAUCE

¼ CUP JAGGERY

2 MAKRUT LIME LEAVES

1 CARROT, PEELED AND JULIENNED

2 CUPS SPINACH

¾ LB. EXTRA-FIRM TOFU, DRAINED AND CHOPPED

DIRECTIONS

1. Place the oil in a large saucepan and warm over medium heat. When the oil starts to shimmer, add the onion, garlic, and curry powder and cook until the onion starts to soften, about 5 minutes.

2. Add the stock, chili pepper, lime zest and juice, soy sauce, jaggery, and lime leaves. Bring to a boil, reduce the heat so that the soup simmers, and cook for 10 minutes.

3. Add the carrot and continue to simmer for 5 minutes. Add the spinach and tofu just prior to serving. Stir to combine, season with salt and pepper, and ladle into warmed bowls.

Dried Fava Bean Soup with Grilled Halloumi Cheese

YIELD: **4 SERVINGS**

ACTIVE TIME: **30 MINUTES**

TOTAL TIME: **24 HOURS**

Halloumi cheese's ability to stand up to high heat allows it to spruce up this humble bean soup without requiring much additional effort from you.

INGREDIENTS

1½ CUPS DRIED FAVA BEANS, SOAKED OVERNIGHT

6 CUPS VEGETABLE STOCK (SEE PAGE 12)

4 GARLIC CLOVES, MINCED

5 TABLESPOONS OLIVE OIL

1 SHALLOT, MINCED

ZEST AND JUICE OF 1 LEMON

SALT AND PEPPER, TO TASTE

2 TABLESPOONS FINELY CHOPPED FRESH PARSLEY

½ LB. HALLOUMI CHEESE, CUT INTO 4 PIECES

LEMON WEDGES, FOR SERVING

DIRECTIONS

1. Drain the fava beans and place them in a large saucepan with the stock and garlic. Bring to a boil, reduce the heat so that the soup simmers, cover, and cook until the beans are so tender that they are falling apart, about 1 hour.

2. While the soup is simmering, place ¼ cup of the olive oil in a skillet and warm over medium heat. Add the shallot and cook until it starts to soften, about 5 minutes. Remove the pan from heat, stir in the lemon zest, and let the mixture sit for 1 hour.

3. Transfer the soup to a food processor and puree until smooth. Return the soup to a clean saucepan, season with salt and pepper, and bring to a gentle simmer.

4. Stir the lemon juice and parsley into the mixture in the skillet and then set it aside.

5. Warm a skillet or a grill pan over medium heat. Place the remaining oil in a small bowl, add the cheese, and toss to coat. Place the cheese in the pan and cook until browned on both sides, about 2 minutes per side. Serve alongside the soup, infused oil, and lemon wedges.

Cream of Mushroom Soup

This soup is quick, but rich. The texture of fusilli is preferred for this preparation, but feel free to swap in your favorite pasta, or whatever happens to be in the cupboard.

YIELD: **4 SERVINGS**

ACTIVE TIME: **30 MINUTES**

TOTAL TIME: **1 HOUR**

INGREDIENTS

4 TABLESPOONS UNSALTED BUTTER

1 ONION, CHOPPED

2 GARLIC CLOVES, CHOPPED

⅓ CUP MADEIRA

¾ LB. WILD MUSHROOMS

4 CUPS MUSHROOM STOCK (SEE PAGE 15)

1½ CUPS FUSILLI PASTA

1 CUP HEAVY CREAM

SALT AND PEPPER, TO TASTE

FRESH PARSLEY, FINELY CHOPPED, FOR GARNISH

DIRECTIONS

1. Place the butter in a large saucepan and melt over medium heat. Add the onion and garlic and cook until the onion starts to soften, about 5 minutes.

2. Add the Madeira and cook until it has evaporated, about 5 minutes. Add the mushrooms and cook until they have released all of their liquid and start to brown, about 10 minutes.

3. Add the stock and bring to a boil. Reduce heat so that the soup simmers and cook for 10 minutes.

4. Transfer the soup to a food processor or blender, puree until smooth and creamy, and then strain through a fine sieve.

5. Return the soup to a clean pan and bring to a simmer. Add the fusilli and cook until it is tender, about 8 minutes.

6. Add the heavy cream and simmer for 2 minutes while stirring constantly. Season with salt and pepper, ladle into warmed bowls, and garnish with parsley.

Portobello Mushroom Ravioli in Beet Soup

YIELD: **4 SERVINGS**

ACTIVE TIME: **1 HOUR**

TOTAL TIME: **1 HOUR AND 45 MINUTES**

Once you get some practice with making ravioli, try making some into heart shapes to serve a loved one—they'll look great in the vibrant beet soup.

INGREDIENTS

FOR THE RAVIOLI

1 CUP "00" FLOUR, PLUS MORE FOR DUSTING

1 PINCH KOSHER SALT, PLUS MORE TO TASTE

1 CUP BEATEN EGG YOLKS

1 TEASPOON OLIVE OIL

1 TABLESPOON UNSALTED BUTTER

2 CUPS CHOPPED PORTOBELLO MUSHROOMS

1 SHALLOT, MINCED

1 GARLIC CLOVE, MINCED

LEAVES FROM 1 SPRIG FRESH THYME, CHOPPED

2 TABLESPOONS MASCARPONE CHEESE

BLACK PEPPER, TO TASTE

1 EGG, BEATEN

1 TABLESPOON WATER

Continued...

DIRECTIONS

1. To begin preparations for the ravioli, combine the flour and salt in a mixing bowl and make a well in the center. Place the egg yolks and the olive oil in the well and slowly incorporate the flour until the dough holds together. Knead the dough until smooth, about 5 minutes. Cover the bowl with plastic wrap and let stand at room temperature for 30 minutes.

2. Place the butter in a medium saucepan and melt over medium heat. Add the mushrooms and cook until they start to release their liquid, about 5 minutes. Add the shallot, garlic, and thyme and cook until the shallot starts to soften, about 5 minutes. Remove the pan from heat and strain the mixture to remove any excess liquid. Let the mixture cool. Once it is cool, place in a small bowl and add the mascarpone. Stir to combine, season with salt and pepper, and set the filling aside.

3. To begin forming the ravioli, divide the dough into two pieces. Use a pasta maker to roll each piece into a long, thin rectangle. Place one of the rectangles over a floured ravioli tray and spoon a teaspoon of the filling in each of the depressions. Combine the beaten egg and water in a small bowl. Dip a pastry brush or a finger into it the wash and lightly coat the edges of each ravioli.

4. Gently lay the other rectangle over the piece in the ravioli tray. Use a rolling pin to gently cut out the ravioli. Remove the cut ravioli and place them on a flour-dusted baking sheet.

Continued...

FOR THE SOUP

1 TABLESPOON OLIVE OIL

1 ONION, CHOPPED

2 GARLIC CLOVES, MINCED

1 TEASPOON FENNEL SEEDS

1 LARGE BEET, PEELED AND MINCED

6 CUPS VEGETABLE STOCK (SEE PAGE 12)

¼ CUP ORANGE JUICE

SALT AND PEPPER, TO TASTE

5. To begin preparations for the soup, place the oil in a large saucepan and warm over medium heat. When the oil starts to shimmer, add the onion, garlic, and fennel seeds and cook until the onion starts to soften, about 5 minutes. Add the beet and cook for 5 minutes. Add the stock and orange juice, bring to a boil, then reduce heat so that the soup simmers. Cook until the beet is tender, about 15 minutes. Transfer the soup to a blender, puree until smooth, and return to the saucepan.

6. Season with salt and pepper and return to a boil. Once boiling, drop the ravioli into the pan and cook for 3 minutes. Ladle the soup and ravioli into shallow bowls.

Spicy Baby Spinach & Rice Soup

YIELD: **4 SERVINGS**

ACTIVE TIME: **15 MINUTES**

TOTAL TIME: **45 MINUTES**

This delicacy is perfect for a spring or summer day, and can easily accommodate any other vegetables you'd like to include.

INGREDIENTS

2 TABLESPOONS WATER

12 CUPS BABY SPINACH

3 TABLESPOONS OLIVE OIL

1 SMALL ONION, CHOPPED

2 GARLIC CLOVES, MINCED

1 SMALL RED CHILI PEPPER, STEMMED, SEEDED, AND MINCED

4 CUPS VEGETABLE STOCK (SEE PAGE 12)

⅓ CUP ARBORIO RICE

SALT AND PEPPER, TO TASTE

ROMANO CHEESE, GRATED, FOR GARNISH

DIRECTIONS

1. Place the water and spinach in a large saucepan and cook over medium-high heat until the spinach has wilted, about 5 minutes. Drain, allow the spinach to cool, and then mince it.

2. Place the oil in a large saucepan and warm over medium heat. When it starts to shimmer, add the onion, garlic, and chili pepper and cook until the onion starts to soften, about 5 minutes.

3. Add the stock and stir in the rice. Bring to a boil, reduce heat so that the soup simmers, and cook until the rice is nearly tender, about 15 minutes.

4. Return the spinach to the pan and cook until the rice is completely tender, about 5 minutes. Season with salt and pepper, ladle into warmed bowls, and garnish with the Romano cheese.

French Lentil Soup

YIELD: **4 TO 6 SERVINGS**

ACTIVE TIME: **25 MINUTES**

TOTAL TIME: **1 HOUR AND 15 MINUTES**

This traditional French soup is sure to warm the bones on a raw winter day.

INGREDIENTS

2 TABLESPOONS OLIVE OIL

1 ONION, CHOPPED

1 GARLIC CLOVE, MINCED

1 CARROT, PEELED AND MINCED

1 LEEK, TRIMMED, RINSED WELL, AND MINCED

1 CELERY STALK, MINCED

1 TABLESPOON TOMATO PASTE

1½ CUPS FRENCH LENTILS

6 CUPS VEGETABLE STOCK (SEE PAGE 12)

1 SACHET D'EPICES (SEE SIDEBAR)

1 BAY LEAF

LEAVES FROM 2 SPRIGS THYME, FINELY CHOPPED

¼ TEASPOON CARAWAY SEEDS

½ LEMON, SLICED

1 TABLESPOON APPLE CIDER VINEGAR

¼ CUP RIESLING

SALT AND PEPPER, TO TASTE

DIRECTIONS

1. Place the oil in a large saucepan and warm over medium heat. When the oil starts to shimmer, add the onion and garlic and cook until the onion starts to soften, about 5 minutes. Add the carrot, leek, and celery and cook until they start to soften, about 5 minutes.

2. Add the tomato paste and cook, while stirring, for 2 minutes. Add the lentils, stock, Sachet d'Epices, bay leaf, thyme, caraway seeds, and lemon slices. Bring to a boil, reduce heat so that the soup simmers, and cook until the lentils are tender, about 30 minutes.

3. Remove the Sachet d'Epices and lemon slices from the soup. Stir in the vinegar and Riesling, season with salt and pepper, and ladle into warmed bowls.

SACHET D'EPICES

Getting familiar with this handy little spice sack will save you time in a number of preparations. Place 3 sprigs of fresh parsley, 1 sprig of fresh thyme, ½ bay leaf, ¼ teaspoon cracked peppercorns, and ½ garlic clove in a 4-inch square of cheesecloth and fold the corners together to make a purse. Tie it closed with a length of kitchen twine, tie the other end of the twine to the handle of your saucepan, and drop the sachet into the soup or dish.

Vegetable Soup with Couscous

YIELD: **4 TO 6 SERVINGS**

ACTIVE TIME: **15 MINUTES**

TOTAL TIME: **35 MINUTES**

Adding the toasted goodness of Israeli couscous transforms what should be a ho-hum vegetable soup.

INGREDIENTS

2 TABLESPOONS OLIVE OIL

1 ONION, CHOPPED

1 LARGE CARROT, PEELED AND CHOPPED

1 (14 OZ.) CAN DICED TOMATOES

5 GARLIC CLOVES, MINCED

6 CUPS VEGETABLE STOCK (SEE PAGE 12)

1¼ CUPS ISRAELI COUSCOUS

¼ TEASPOON CUMIN

3 TABLESPOONS FINELY CHOPPED FRESH CILANTRO

SALT AND PEPPER, TO TASTE

⅛ TEASPOON CAYENNE PEPPER

DIRECTIONS

1. Place the oil in a large saucepan and warm over medium heat. When the oil starts to shimmer, add the onion and carrot and cook until they start to soften, about 5 minutes.

2. Add the remaining ingredients. Bring to a boil, reduce heat so that the soup simmers, and cook until the couscous is tender, about 5 minutes. Ladle into warmed bowls and serve.

YIELD: **4 TO 6 SERVINGS**

ACTIVE TIME: **20 MINUTES**

TOTAL TIME: **45 MINUTES**

Vegan Curried Laksa Soup

A lovely soup that is worth preparing if only to ensure that you have some extra Laksa Curry Paste sitting around afterward.

INGREDIENTS

1 TABLESPOON OLIVE OIL

LAKSA CURRY PASTE (SEE SIDEBAR)

2 CUPS SLICED SHIITAKE MUSHROOMS

2 CARROTS, PEELED AND SLICED

¼ CUP CHOPPED RED BELL PEPPERS

¼ CUP CHOPPED GREEN BELL PEPPERS

¼ CUP CHOPPED ZUCCHINI

¼ CUP CHOPPED YELLOW SQUASH

4 CUPS VEGETABLE STOCK (SEE PAGE 12)

1 (14 OZ.) CAN COCONUT MILK

½ LB. RICE NOODLES

1 CUP CHOPPED KALE

½ LB. EXTRA-FIRM TOFU, DRAINED AND CHOPPED

1 TABLESPOON SOY SAUCE

1 TABLESPOON FRESH LIME JUICE

1 TEASPOON SUGAR

SALT AND PEPPER, TO TASTE

2 BIRD'S EYE CHILI PEPPERS, STEMMED, SEEDED, AND SLICED, FOR GARNISH

FRESH CILANTRO, FINELY CHOPPED, FOR GARNISH

DIRECTIONS

1. Place the oil in a large saucepan and warm over medium heat. When the oil starts to shimmer, add the Laksa Curry Paste and cook for 3 minutes, while stirring constantly.

2. Add the mushrooms and cook for 2 minutes. Add the carrots, bell peppers, zucchini, and yellow squash and cook until they start to soften, about 5 minutes.

3. Add the stock and coconut milk and bring to a boil. Reduce heat so that the soup simmers, add the noodles, and cook for 10 minutes.

4. Fold in the kale and tofu, simmer for 2 minutes, and then add the soy sauce, lime juice, and sugar. Season with salt and pepper, ladle into warmed bowls, and garnish with the chilies and cilantro.

LAKSA CURRY PASTE

Place 2 teaspoons coriander seeds and ½ teaspoon fennel seeds in a dry skillet and toast until fragrant, about 2 minutes, making sure they don't burn. Place the seeds in a food processor along with 1 teaspoon turmeric, 1 tablespoon minced fresh ginger, 1 seeded and chopped green chili pepper, ½ teaspoon cayenne pepper, 1 lemongrass stalk, 2 garlic cloves, 2 tablespoons cashews, ½ cup finely chopped fresh cilantro, 1 teaspoon fresh lime juice, and 2 tablespoons water. Blitz until the mixture is a paste and season with salt and pepper.

INGREDIENTS

FOR THE SOUP

2 TABLESPOONS OLIVE OIL

1 ONION, CHOPPED

2 GARLIC CLOVES, MINCED

1 HEAD CAULIFLOWER, TRIMMED AND CHOPPED

4 CUPS VEGETABLE STOCK (SEE PAGE 12)

¾ CUP QUINOA, RINSED

LEAVES FROM 2 SPRIGS FRESH THYME, FINELY CHOPPED

½ CUP HEAVY CREAM

SALT AND PEPPER, TO TASTE

FRESH CHIVES, FINELY CHOPPED, FOR GARNISH

FOR THE CRISPY CAULIFLOWER

1 CUP VEGETABLE OIL

4 CUPS WATER

1 TEASPOON KOSHER SALT, PLUS MORE TO TASTE

12 SMALL CAULIFLOWER FLORETS

¾ CUP ALL-PURPOSE FLOUR

¼ CUP CORNSTARCH

½ TEASPOON BAKING POWDER

1 CUP SODA WATER

BLACK PEPPER, TO TASTE

Cauliflower & Quinoa Soup

YIELD: **4 SERVINGS**

ACTIVE TIME: **30 MINUTES**

TOTAL TIME: **1 HOUR**

The crunch of the cauliflower, the chewiness of the quinoa, and the creamy broth give this soup a great texture.

DIRECTIONS

1. To begin preparations for the soup, place the oil in a large saucepan and warm over medium heat. When the oil starts to shimmer, add the onion and cook until it starts to soften, about 5 minutes.

2. Add the garlic and cook until fragrant, about 2 minutes. Add the cauliflower, stock, quinoa, and thyme and bring to a boil. Reduce heat so that the soup simmers, cover the pan, and cook until the cauliflower and quinoa are tender, about 15 minutes.

3. While the soup is simmering, begin preparations for the crispy cauliflower. Place the oil in a Dutch oven and bring it to 350°F. Prepare an ice water bath in a mixing bowl. Place the water and salt in a small saucepan and bring to a boil. Add the cauliflower, cook for 3 minutes, and transfer to the ice water bath. When the cauliflower is cool, set it on paper towels to drain.

4. Sift ½ cup of the flour, the cornstarch, and baking powder into a mixing bowl. Add the soda water and whisk until smooth. Place the remaining flour and the cauliflower in a small bowl and toss until the florets are evenly coated.

5. Dip each piece of cauliflower in the batter and then place them in the oil. Fry until golden brown, remove with a slotted spoon, and set on a paper towel-lined plate to drain. Season with salt and pepper and let cool slightly.

6. Stir the heavy cream into the soup, season with salt and pepper, and ladle into warmed bowls. Serve with the crispy cauliflower and garnish with the chives.

CHAPTER 5

SIDES

———

The space where vegetables have always shined. Just think about the Thanksgiving table, and how often people's sunny memories of that day center less upon the turkey than those unique recipes that tend to flank the bird.

From the smoky richness of the Patatas Bravas (see page 168) beloved by the people of Spain, a Potato & Celeriac Gratin with Gruyère & Figs (see page 199) so good that it's worthy of being passed down through the generations, and three preparations for that gem of spring, asparagus, you can be certain that every plate coming out of your kitchen will be freighted with flavor.

Patatas Bravas

YIELD: 4 SERVINGS

ACTIVE TIME: 25 MINUTES

TOTAL TIME: 1 HOUR AND 15 MINUTES

Native to Spain, this smoky potato dish can be found in tapas bars all across that country.

INGREDIENTS

2 CUPS WOOD CHIPS

4 POTATOES, CHOPPED

1 ONION, WITH SKIN AND ROOT, HALVED

3 TABLESPOONS OLIVE OIL

1 HEAD GARLIC, TOP ½ INCH REMOVED

1 (14 OZ.) CAN DICED TOMATOES, DRAINED

1 TABLESPOON SWEET PAPRIKA

1 TABLESPOON SHERRY VINEGAR

SALT, TO TASTE

SOUR CREAM, FOR SERVING

DIRECTIONS

1. Place the wood chips in a bowl of cold water and let them soak for 30 minutes.

2. Bring water to a boil in a large saucepan. Add the potatoes and boil for 4 minutes. Drain and run the potatoes under cold water.

3. Place the potatoes, onion, and 1 tablespoon of the olive oil in a mixing bowl and toss to coat.

4. Line a large wok with aluminum foil, making sure that the foil extends over the side of the pan. Add the soaked wood chips and place the wok over medium heat.

5. When the wood chips are smoking heavily, place a wire rack above the wood chips and place the potatoes, onion, and garlic on top. Cover the wok with a lid, fold the foil over the lid to seal the wok as best you can, and smoke the vegetables for 20 minutes. After 20 minutes, remove the pan from heat and keep the wok covered for another 20 minutes.

6. Place the tomatoes, paprika, vinegar, and remaining olive oil in a blender and puree until smooth. Set the mixture aside.

7. Remove the garlic and onion from the smoker. Peel and roughly chop. Add to the mixture in the blender and puree until smooth. Season the salsa brava with salt and serve alongside the potatoes and sour cream.

Garlic & Chili Broccolini

YIELD: **4 SERVINGS**

ACTIVE TIME: **10 MINUTES**

TOTAL TIME: **30 MINUTES**

You can also use broccoli in this dish, but the sweeter flavor of broccolini is a better match for the spice.

INGREDIENTS

SALT AND PEPPER, TO TASTE

½ LB. BROCCOLINI, ENDS TRIMMED

¼ CUP OLIVE OIL

2 GARLIC CLOVES, MINCED

1 TEASPOON RED PEPPER FLAKES

2 TABLESPOONS ALMONDS, TOASTED, FOR GARNISH

DIRECTIONS

1. Bring a large pot of salted water to a boil. Add the broccolini and cook for 30 seconds. Remove with a strainer, allow the majority of the water to drip off, and transfer to a paper towel–lined plate.

2. Place the olive oil in a large skillet and warm over medium-high heat.

3. When the oil starts to shimmer, add the broccolini and cook until it is well browned, about 6 minutes. Turn the broccolini over, add the garlic, season with salt and pepper, and toss to combine. When the broccolini is browned all over, add the red pepper flakes and toss to evenly distribute.

4. Transfer to a serving platter and garnish with the toasted almonds.

Asparagus, Three Ways

YIELD: **4 SERVINGS**

ACTIVE TIME: **10 MINUTES**

TOTAL TIME: **15 TO 25 MINUTES**

As there are so many options when working with asparagus, the basics for cooking it three ways are provided, and each is as delectable as the next.

INGREDIENTS

1½ LBS. ASPARAGUS

SALT, TO TASTE

OLIVE OIL, AS NEEDED

BLENDER HOLLANDAISE (SEE PAGE 19), FOR SERVING (OPTIONAL)

TAHINI DRESSING (SEE PAGE 20), FOR SERVING (OPTIONAL)

DIRECTIONS

1. Begin every preparation for asparagus by rinsing the spears well under cold water. Take a spear and bend it close to the end that is opposite the pointy tip; it will snap off at the point where it starts to be too fibrous and tough to eat. Discard any fibrous ends, or reserve for another preparation.

2. To blanch asparagus, cook the spears in salted, boiling water until just tender, about 3 minutes. Transfer immediately to an ice water bath to retain the green color.

3. To steam asparagus, arrange the spears in a steaming tray, place the tray above 1 inch of boiling water, and steam for roughly 5 minutes. Transfer immediately to an ice water bath to retain the bright green color.

4. To grill asparagus, preheat your grill to medium-high heat. Place the asparagus in a bowl, drizzle some olive oil over it, and sprinkle with salt. Toss to coat, place the asparagus on the grill, and cook until it just starts to char, about 4 minutes. Turn over, cook for another 4 minutes, then transfer to a plate.

5. Serve any of these preparations with your sauce of choice and season to taste.

Corn Fritters

YIELD: **4 SERVINGS**

ACTIVE TIME: **20 MINUTES**

TOTAL TIME: **40 MINUTES**

Sweet yet substantive, fancy yet simple, corn fritters are a family chef's best friend because they work no matter what the occasion.

INGREDIENTS

1 EGG, BEATEN

1 TEASPOON SUGAR

½ TEASPOON KOSHER SALT

1 TABLESPOON UNSALTED BUTTER, MELTED

2 TEASPOONS BAKING POWDER

1 CUP ALL-PURPOSE FLOUR

⅔ CUP MILK

2 CUPS COOKED CORN, AT ROOM TEMPERATURE

2 TABLESPOONS CANOLA OIL

DIRECTIONS

1. Place the egg, sugar, salt, butter, baking powder, flour, and milk in a mixing bowl and stir until thoroughly combined. Add the corn and stir to incorporate.

2. Place the oil in a 12-inch cast-iron skillet and warm over medium-high heat. When the oil starts to shimmer, drop heaping spoonfuls of batter into the skillet and gently press down to flatten them into disks. Make sure not to crowd the pan. Cook until the fritters are browned on both sides, about 3 minutes per side. Transfer to a paper towel–lined plate and tent with aluminum foil to keep warm while you cook the rest of the fritters. Serve once all of the fritters have been cooked.

TIP: The best corn to use for this is leftover cooked corn on the cob that's been in the refrigerator overnight. Otherwise, you can take frozen corn and thaw the kernels, drying them before putting them in the batter. If you use canned corn, be sure all water is drained from it, and choose a high-quality brand so the kernels are firm and sweet, not mushy.

Charred Onion Petals

YIELD: **4 SERVINGS**

ACTIVE TIME: **10 MINUTES**

TOTAL TIME: **1 HOUR**

An easy-to-master and utterly beautiful preparation that makes for a stunning side dish. Make sure to use sweet onions, though, since the flavor of yellow onions will be too sharp. These are just as good cold, so don't hesitate to make a batch ahead of time.

INGREDIENTS

3 VIDALIA ONIONS

2 TABLESPOONS OLIVE OIL

SALT, TO TASTE

DIRECTIONS

1. Preheat the oven to 300°F.

2. Cut each onion in half lengthwise and remove the outer layer.

3. Place a 12-inch cast-iron skillet over high heat and add the olive oil. When the oil starts to shimmer, place the onions, cut-side down, in the pan. Reduce heat to medium-low and cook until the onions are charred, about 20 minutes. They will smell burnt, but don't worry.

4. Place the skillet in the oven and roast until the onions are tender, 10 to 15 minutes. Remove the skillet from the oven and let the onions cool.

5. When the onions are cool enough to handle, use kitchen scissors to trim the tops and roots. Discard and separate the layers into individual petals. Season with salt and serve.

Potato & Tomato Tart

YIELD: **4 TO 6 SERVINGS**

ACTIVE TIME: **15 MINUTES**

TOTAL TIME: **1 HOUR**

A testament to the brilliance of French cuisine, this layered dish has all the flavor in the world and is as simple as can be to make.

INGREDIENTS

4 GARLIC CLOVES, MINCED

LEAVES FROM 1 SMALL BUNCH PARSLEY, FINELY CHOPPED

2 TABLESPOONS FINELY CHOPPED FRESH THYME

OLIVE OIL, TO TASTE

2 LBS. TOMATOES, SLICED ¼ INCH THICK

SALT AND PEPPER, TO TASTE

4 YUKON GOLD POTATOES, SLICED ¼ INCH THICK

VEGETABLE STOCK (SEE PAGE 12), AS NEEDED

DIRECTIONS

1. Preheat the oven to 350°F. Place the garlic, parsley, and thyme in a small bowl, stir to combine, and set the mixture aside while you prepare the tomatoes.

2. Lightly grease a 12-inch cast-iron skillet or an enameled gratin dish with olive oil and then add a layer of the tomato slices. Season with salt and pepper and add a layer of potatoes and some of the garlic-and-parsley mixture. Drizzle with olive oil and continue the layering process until all of the tomatoes, potatoes, and garlic-and-parsley mixture have been used.

3. Cover the skillet or gratin dish with aluminum foil, place it in the oven, and bake for 20 minutes. Remove from the oven and uncover the skillet or dish. If tomatoes haven't released enough liquid to soften the potatoes, add a bit of stock. Replace the foil and continue baking for 15 minutes.

4. Remove the foil and cook for an additional 5 minutes. Remove from the oven and briefly let cool before serving.

Winter Tomatoes with Thyme

YIELD: **4 TO 6 SERVINGS**

ACTIVE TIME: **5 MINUTES**

TOTAL TIME: **1 HOUR**

Chances are, the tomatoes in your area aren't at their peak during winter. But that doesn't mean you have to cross them off your list, as this slow-roasted version will draw out the flavor you're craving.

INGREDIENTS

1 CUP OLIVE OIL

12 ROMA TOMATOES, CONCASSE (SEE PAGE 37)

12 GARLIC CLOVES, CHOPPED

6 SPRIGS FRESH THYME

DIRECTIONS

1. Preheat the oven to 300°F. Place the olive oil in a Dutch oven and warm over medium-low heat. When the oil starts to shimmer, add the tomatoes and cook, without stirring, for 3 minutes. Add the garlic and thyme and toss to combine.

2. Cover the Dutch oven and place it in the oven. Roast until the tomatoes and garlic are extremely tender, about 45 minutes. Remove and let cool.

3. Remove the sprigs of thyme and discard them before serving.

Mom's Creamed Spinach

Make sure you use frozen spinach for this one, as fresh will wilt and leave you with far less than the amount you need to bring to the table.

YIELD: **4 SERVINGS**

ACTIVE TIME: **20 MINUTES**

TOTAL TIME: **25 MINUTES**

INGREDIENTS

1 TABLESPOON UNSALTED BUTTER

1 YELLOW ONION, CHOPPED

2 GARLIC CLOVES, CHOPPED

1 LB. FROZEN CHOPPED SPINACH

½ LB. CREAM CHEESE, AT ROOM TEMPERATURE

1 PINCH GROUND NUTMEG

1 TEASPOON MARJORAM

SALT AND PEPPER, TO TASTE

DIRECTIONS

1. Place the butter in a skillet and melt over medium heat. Add the onion and garlic and cook until the onion is translucent, about 3 minutes.

2. Add the frozen spinach to the pan along with a few teaspoons of water, cover the pan, and cook for 4 minutes. Remove the lid, break the spinach up, and cook until it is completely thawed.

3. Add the cream cheese, nutmeg, and marjoram and stir to incorporate. Cook until the sauce has reduced and thickened, about 5 minutes. Season with salt and pepper and serve.

Polenta Fries

Frying strips of polenta is a great way to take advantage of its creamy texture and beautiful golden hue.

YIELD: **4 SERVINGS**

ACTIVE TIME: **30 MINUTES**

TOTAL TIME: **2 HOURS AND 30 MINUTES**

INGREDIENTS

2½ CUPS MILK

2½ CUPS VEGETABLE STOCK (SEE PAGE 12)

2 CUPS MEDIUM-GRAIN CORNMEAL

2 TABLESPOONS UNSALTED BUTTER

1 TEASPOON KOSHER SALT, PLUS MORE TO TASTE

½ TEASPOON BLACK PEPPER

½ TEASPOON DRIED OREGANO

½ TEASPOON DRIED THYME

½ TEASPOON DRIED ROSEMARY

4 CUPS VEGETABLE OIL

¼ CUP GRATED PARMESAN CHEESE, FOR GARNISH

2 TABLESPOONS FINELY CHOPPED FRESH ROSEMARY, FOR GARNISH

DIRECTIONS

1. Grease a large, rimmed baking sheet with nonstick cooking spray. Place the milk and stock in a saucepan and bring to a boil. Whisk in the polenta, reduce heat to low, and cook, while stirring constantly, until all of the liquid has been absorbed and the polenta is creamy, about 5 minutes.

2. Stir in the butter, salt, pepper, oregano, thyme, and dried rosemary. When they have been incorporated, transfer the polenta to the greased baking sheet and even out the surface with a rubber spatula. Refrigerate for 2 hours.

3. Carefully invert the baking sheet over a cutting board so that the polenta falls onto it. Slice in half lengthwise and cut each piece into 4-inch-long and 1-inch-wide strips.

4. Place the oil in a Dutch oven and bring it to 375°F. Working in batches of two, place the strips in the oil and fry, turning as they cook, until golden brown, 2 to 4 minutes. Transfer the cooked fries to a paper towel–lined plate to drain. When all of the fries have been cooked, sprinkle the Parmesan and fresh rosemary over them and serve.

Confit New Potatoes

New potatoes are sweeter than their mature counterparts, since their sugars haven't had time to develop into starches, and are so soft and tender that they don't need to be peeled.

YIELD: **4 TO 6 SERVINGS**

ACTIVE TIME: **5 MINUTES**

TOTAL TIME: **1 HOUR AND 15 MINUTES**

INGREDIENTS

4 CUPS VEGETABLE OIL

5 LBS. NEW POTATOES

SALT AND PEPPER, TO TASTE

DIRECTIONS

1. Place the oil in a Dutch oven and bring it to 200°F over medium heat.

2. While the oil is warming, wash the potatoes and pat them dry. Carefully place the potatoes in the oil and cook until fork-tender, about 1 hour.

3. Drain the potatoes, season generously with salt and pepper, and stir to ensure that the potatoes are evenly coated.

Grilled Corn with Chipotle Mayonnaise & Goat Cheese

YIELD: **6 SERVINGS**

ACTIVE TIME: **25 MINUTES**

TOTAL TIME: **1 HOUR AND 15 MINUTES**

This dish has it all—sweet corn, spice from the chipotle, and a soft, creamy landing thanks to the goat cheese.

INGREDIENTS

6 EARS CORN, IN THEIR HUSKS

3 CHIPOTLES IN ADOBO

½ CUP MAYONNAISE

¼ CUP SOUR CREAM

1½ TABLESPOONS BROWN SUGAR

1 TABLESPOON FRESH LIME JUICE

2 TABLESPOONS FINELY CHOPPED FRESH CILANTRO, PLUS MORE FOR GARNISH

1 TEASPOON KOSHER SALT, PLUS MORE TO TASTE

½ TEASPOON BLACK PEPPER, PLUS MORE TO TASTE

3 TABLESPOONS OLIVE OIL

½ CUP CRUMBLED GOAT CHEESE

6 LIME WEDGES, FOR SERVING

DIRECTIONS

1. Preheat the oven to 400°F. Place the ears of corn on a baking sheet, place it in the oven, and roast for 25 minutes, until the kernels have a slight give to them. Remove from the oven and let cool. When the ears of corn are cool enough to handle, remove the husks.

2. Preheat your gas or charcoal grill to 400°F. Place the chipotles, mayonnaise, sour cream, brown sugar, lime juice, cilantro, salt, and pepper in a food processor and puree until smooth. Set aside.

3. Drizzle the ears of corn with the olive oil, season with salt and pepper, and place them on the grill. Cook, while turning, until they are charred all over, about 10 minutes.

4. Spread the mayonnaise on the ears of corn, sprinkle the goat cheese over the top, and garnish with additional cilantro. Serve with wedges of lime.

CRÈME FRAÎCHE

You can find crème fraiche at the store, but as it is typically expensive and very easy to make at home, it's better to handle it yourself. Simply combine 1 cup heavy cream and 1 tablespoon of buttermilk in a mason jar, cover it, and let stand at room temperature for 12 hours. Use immediately or store in the refrigerator for up to 1 month.

Honey Roasted Turnips with Hazelnuts

YIELD: **4 TO 6 SERVINGS**

ACTIVE TIME: **15 MINUTES**

TOTAL TIME: **40 MINUTES**

Try to make this with the smallest turnips you can find, with Japanese turnips topping the list of desirable varieties.

INGREDIENTS

16 SMALL TURNIPS, TRIMMED AND QUARTERED

¼ CUP OLIVE OIL

½ CUP HONEY

SALT AND PEPPER, TO TASTE

¾ CUP CRÈME FRAÎCHE (SEE SIDEBAR)

¼ CUP THINLY SLICED FRESH CHIVES

ZEST AND JUICE OF 1 LEMON

½ CUP HAZELNUTS, TOASTED AND CHOPPED

DIRECTIONS

1. Preheat the oven to 350°F.

2. Warm a large cast-iron skillet over medium-high heat for 5 minutes, until it is very hot.

3. Place the turnips, olive oil, and honey in a large bowl, season with salt and pepper, and toss to coat. Place the turnips in the skillet, cut-side down, and transfer the skillet to the oven. Roast until tender, about 30 minutes.

4. While the turnips are roasting, place the Crème Fraîche, chives, lemon zest, and lemon juice in a bowl and whisk to combine. Season with salt and pepper and set aside.

5. To serve, sprinkle the hazelnuts over the turnips and drizzle the Crème Fraîche mixture over the top.

Blistered Shishito Peppers

YIELD: **4 TO 6 SERVINGS**

ACTIVE TIME: **10 MINUTES**

TOTAL TIME: **20 MINUTES**

Eating shishito peppers is a bit like putting your taste buds through a round of Russian roulette, since approximately one in every 10 is spicy, and there's no way to tell until you bite down. The rest are as mild as can be.

INGREDIENTS

OLIVE OIL, FOR FRYING

2 LBS. SHISHITO PEPPERS

SALT, TO TASTE

LEMON WEDGES, FOR SERVING

DIRECTIONS

1. Add olive oil to a 12-inch cast-iron skillet until it is ¼ inch deep and warm over medium heat.

2. When the oil is shimmering, add the peppers and cook, while turning once or twice, until they are blistered and golden brown, about 2 minutes. Take care not to crowd the pan with the peppers, and work in batches if necessary.

3. Transfer the blistered peppers to a paper towel–lined plate. Season with salt and serve with lemon wedges.

Fried Brussels Sprouts with Maple-Cider Glaze

YIELD: **4 SERVINGS**

ACTIVE TIME: **10 MINUTES**

TOTAL TIME: **15 MINUTES**

Don't limit this sweet-and-tangy glaze to this preparation, as it can confidently be applied to any brassica or root vegetable.

INGREDIENTS

¾ CUP REAL MAPLE SYRUP

½ CUP APPLE CIDER VINEGAR

½ CUP APPLE CIDER

SALT, TO TASTE

VEGETABLE OIL, FOR FRYING

1 LB. BRUSSELS SPROUTS, TRIMMED AND HALVED

DIRECTIONS

1. Place the maple syrup, vinegar, apple cider, and a pinch of salt in a saucepan and cook, stirring constantly, over medium heat until it has reduced by one-quarter. Remove from heat and set aside.

2. Add oil to a Dutch oven until it is about 3 inches deep. Bring to 350°F, place the Brussels sprouts in the oil, and fry until they are crispy and browned, about 1 to 2 minutes. Transfer to a paper towel–lined plate to drain.

3. Place the Brussels sprouts in a bowl, season with salt, and add 1 tablespoon of the glaze for every cup of Brussels sprouts. Toss until evenly coated and serve.

   TIP: If you prefer not to deep-fry the Brussels sprouts, toss them with oil and salt and roast at 375°F for 20 minutes, until the Brussels sprouts are tender but still have a bite to them.

Basic Red Cabbage Slaw

YIELD: **4 SERVINGS**

ACTIVE TIME: **5 MINUTES**

TOTAL TIME: **2 HOURS AND 15 MINUTES**

The longer you can let this sit, the better. When it's ready, the cabbage will have softened and you'll have the perfect topper for taco night.

INGREDIENTS

1 SMALL RED CABBAGE, CORED AND SLICED VERY THIN

1 TEASPOON KOSHER SALT, PLUS MORE TO TASTE

JUICE OF 1 LIME

1 BUNCH FRESH CILANTRO, FINELY CHOPPED

DIRECTIONS

1. Place the cabbage in a large bowl, sprinkle the salt on top, and toss to distribute. Use your hands to work the salt into the cabbage, then let it sit for at least 2 hours.

2. Once the cabbage has rested, taste to gauge the saltiness: if too salty, rinse under cold water and drain; if just right, add the lime juice and cilantro, stir to combine, and serve.

Potato & Celeriac Gratin with Gruyère & Figs

YIELD: **4 SERVINGS**

ACTIVE TIME: **45 MINUTES**

TOTAL TIME: **1 HOUR AND 30 MINUTES**

Parboiling the potatoes and celeriac before placing them in the casserole dish adds flavor and also ensures everything will be cooked through in the oven.

INGREDIENTS

1½ LBS. RUSSET POTATOES, PEELED AND SLICED THIN

½ LB. CELERIAC, PEELED, TRIMMED, AND SLICED THIN

1 BAY LEAF

2 TEASPOONS KOSHER SALT

2 GARLIC CLOVES, CRUSHED

2 TABLESPOONS MILK

1 TABLESPOON UNSALTED BUTTER

3 FRESH OR DRIED FIGS, DICED

4 OZ. GRUYÈRE CHEESE, GRATED

GROUND NUTMEG, TO TASTE

½ CUP HEAVY CREAM

DIRECTIONS

1. Preheat the oven to 375°F. Place the potatoes and celeriac in a medium saucepan and cover with water. Add the bay leaf, 1 teaspoon of the salt, the garlic, and milk, bring to a boil, and then reduce the heat to medium-low. Simmer for 1 minute and drain. Remove the bay leaf and discard.

2. Butter a 10-inch oval gratin dish or a casserole dish and add half of the potatoes and celeriac, making sure they are evenly distributed. Sprinkle half of the figs, some salt, half of the Gruyère, and some nutmeg on top. Repeat with the remaining potatoes and celeriac, seasonings, figs, and Gruyère.

3. Pour the cream over the top and cover the dish with aluminum foil. Place in the oven and bake for 20 minutes. Remove the foil and bake for another 15 minutes, until the top is browned and most of the liquid has cooked off.

4. Remove from the oven and let stand for 15 minutes before serving.

Sautéed Red Cabbage with Apples, Fennel & Balsamic

YIELD: 4 SERVINGS

ACTIVE TIME: 25 MINUTES

TOTAL TIME: 30 MINUTES

This lovely dish is very easy to make vegan by substituting olive oil for the butter.

INGREDIENTS

½ RED CABBAGE, CORED AND SLICED

3 TABLESPOONS UNSALTED BUTTER

¼ CUP WATER

1 APPLE, PEELED, CORED, AND DICED

1 TEASPOON FENNEL SEEDS

SALT AND PEPPER, TO TASTE

2 TABLESPOONS BALSAMIC VINEGAR

DIRECTIONS

1. Place the cabbage in a large skillet with a tablespoon of the butter and the water. Bring to a boil and cover the pan. Let the cabbage steam until the thick ribs are tender, 5 to 8 minutes, then remove the lid and cook until the water has evaporated.

2. Add the remaining butter, the apple, fennel seeds, and a pinch of salt and pepper. Reduce heat to medium-low and cook, stirring occasionally, until the apples and cabbage have caramelized. Stir in the balsamic vinegar and cook for another minute before serving.

Savory Halwa

YIELD: **4 SERVINGS**

ACTIVE TIME: **15 MINUTES**

TOTAL TIME: **20 MINUTES**

Halwa is an Indian dish which is usually prepared as a dessert for special occasions or festivals. This version omits the sugar, but the carrots ensure it is still plenty sweet.

INGREDIENTS

2 TABLESPOONS UNSALTED BUTTER

1 LB. CARROTS, PEELED AND GRATED

½ TEASPOON CARDAMOM

2 CUPS MILK

SALT, TO TASTE

DIRECTIONS

1. Place the butter in a saucepan and melt over medium heat. Add the carrots and cardamom and cook until the carrots start to soften, about 5 minutes.

2. Add the milk, bring to a simmer, and cook until the milk has reduced and the carrots are very tender, about 10 minutes. Season with salt and serve.

Stir-Fried Carrot Noodles

As this rich peanut-and-sesame sauce will find a home in many more dishes than this one, don't hesitate to whip up a double or triple batch.

YIELD: **4 SERVINGS**

ACTIVE TIME: **30 MINUTES**

TOTAL TIME: **30 MINUTES**

INGREDIENTS

2 TEASPOONS SESAME SEEDS

2 TABLESPOONS CREAMY PEANUT BUTTER

2 TABLESPOONS WATER

2 TABLESPOONS RICE VINEGAR

1 TABLESPOON SOY SAUCE

1 TABLESPOON LIGHT BROWN SUGAR

2 TEASPOONS TOASTED SESAME OIL

1 TEASPOON CHILI GARLIC SAUCE, PLUS MORE TO TASTE

1-INCH PIECE FRESH GINGER, PEELED AND GRATED

2 TABLESPOONS PEANUT OIL, PLUS MORE AS NEEDED

4 TO 6 LARGE CARROTS, PEELED AND SPIRALIZED OR GRATED

SALT, TO TASTE

6 SCALLIONS, TRIMMED AND CHOPPED, FOR GARNISH

DIRECTIONS

1. Place the sesame seeds in a small skillet and toast over medium heat until golden brown and aromatic, about 2 minutes. Transfer the sesame seeds to a small bowl and set aside.

2. Place the peanut butter, water, vinegar, soy sauce, brown sugar, sesame oil, chili garlic sauce, and ginger in a small saucepan, whisk to combine, and bring to a gentle boil over medium-low heat. Cook, stirring frequently, until the sauce thickens, 4 to 5 minutes. Remove the sauce from heat and set aside.

3. Warm a wok or a large skillet over medium heat for 2 to 3 minutes. Raise heat to medium-high and add the peanut oil. When the oil starts to shimmer, add half of the carrots and a pinch of salt and stir-fry until the carrots have softened, about 2 minutes. Transfer the carrots to a bowl and set aside. Repeat the process, adding peanut oil if necessary, with the remaining carrots.

4. Add the sauce to the bowl containing the carrots and toss until evenly coated. Garnish with the toasted sesame seeds and the scallions and serve.

Roasted Cauliflower au Gratin

YIELD: **2 SERVINGS**

ACTIVE TIME: **20 MINUTES**

TOTAL TIME: **1 HOUR AND 15 MINUTES**

One surefire way to get people excited about cauliflower is poaching it in a flavorful stock and then caramelizing mild, nutty cheeses like Emmental and Parmesan on top.

INGREDIENTS

2 CUPS WHITE WINE

2½ CUPS WATER

⅓ CUP KOSHER SALT

2 STICKS UNSALTED BUTTER

6 GARLIC CLOVES, CRUSHED

2 SHALLOTS, HALVED

1 CINNAMON STICK

3 WHOLE CLOVES

1 TEASPOON BLACK PEPPERCORNS

1 SPRIG FRESH SAGE

2 SPRIGS FRESH THYME

1 HEAD CAULIFLOWER, LEAVES AND STALK REMOVED

1 CUP SHREDDED EMMENTAL CHEESE

¼ CUP GRATED PARMESAN CHEESE

DIRECTIONS

1. Place all of the ingredients, except for the cauliflower and cheeses, in a large saucepan and bring to a boil. Reduce heat so that the mixture simmers gently, add the head of cauliflower, and poach until tender, about 30 minutes.

2. While the cauliflower is poaching, preheat the oven to 450°F. Transfer the tender cauliflower to a baking sheet, place it in the oven, and bake until the top is a deep golden brown, about 10 minutes.

3. Remove the cauliflower from the oven and spread the cheeses evenly over the top. Return to the oven and bake until the cheeses have browned. Remove from the oven and let cool slightly before cutting the cauliflower in half and serving.

Hot & Garlicky Eggplant Noodles

Eggplants make for good veggie noodles because of their fibrous nature. Use an Italian variety and make sure there is enough room in the pan to fry them; otherwise, they will steam instead of brown.

YIELD: **4 SERVINGS**

ACTIVE TIME: **45 MINUTES**

TOTAL TIME: **45 MINUTES**

INGREDIENTS

4 EGGPLANTS

2 TABLESPOONS CHILI GARLIC SAUCE, PLUS MORE TO TASTE

2 TEASPOONS WATER

3 TABLESPOONS OLIVE OIL

1 TABLESPOON TOASTED SESAME OIL

SALT, TO TASTE

2 HANDFULS FRESH CILANTRO LEAVES, FINELY CHOPPED, FOR GARNISH

½ CUP TAMARI ALMONDS, TOASTED AND CHOPPED, FOR GARNISH

DIRECTIONS

1. Trim the ends of each eggplant and peel them. Using the julienne attachment on a mandoline, carefully cut the eggplants into thin noodles. Alternatively, cut each eggplant into ¼-inch-thick slices, then cut each slice into ¼-inch-wide strips.

2. Place the chili garlic sauce and water in a small bowl and stir until thoroughly combined.

3. Warm a large nonstick skillet over medium heat for 1 minute. Add half of the olive oil, half of the sesame oil, and half of the chili garlic slurry and raise the heat to medium-high. When the oil begins to shimmer, add half of the eggplant noodles and a couple pinches of salt. Cook, stirring frequently, until the strands have softened and start turning golden brown, about 5 minutes. Transfer to a warm plate and tent loosely with foil to keep warm. Wipe out the pan with a paper towel and repeat the process with the remaining eggplant, olive oil, sesame oil, and chili garlic slurry. Garnish with the cilantro and almonds and serve immediately.

Charred Leeks with Romesco Sauce

YIELD: **4 SERVINGS**

ACTIVE TIME: **15 MINUTES**

TOTAL TIME: **30 MINUTES**

When leeks are cooked on a grill, they develop a sweet and smoky flavor. Pairing that sweetness and smoke with a garlicky Romesco sauce is a slice of heaven.

INGREDIENTS

8 LEEKS

OLIVE OIL, TO TASTE

SALT AND PEPPER, TO TASTE

ROMESCO SAUCE (SEE PAGE 23), FOR SERVING

DIRECTIONS

1. Preheat your gas or charcoal grill to 400°F. Cut the dark green sections off of the leeks and remove the roots, keeping the base that holds the layers together. Cut the leeks lengthwise and rinse between each layer to remove dirt, taking care to keep the layers together.

2. Place 1 inch of water in a saucepan, place a steaming tray in the pan, and bring the water to a boil. Place the leeks in the steaming tray, cover, and steam until tender, about 5 minutes.

3. Pat the leeks dry, drizzle oil over them, and season with salt and pepper. When the grill is ready, place the leeks on the grill and cook until browned all over, about 8 minutes per side. When the leeks are charred, transfer to a platter and serve with the Romesco Sauce.

Sautéed Green Beans & Shiitakes

Fresh green beans and the complex, umami-drenched flavor of shiitakes make this simple side seem anything but.

YIELD: **4 SERVINGS**

ACTIVE TIME: **20 MINUTES**

TOTAL TIME: **40 MINUTES**

INGREDIENTS

SALT, TO TASTE

1 LB. GREEN BEANS, CLEANED AND TRIMMED

1 TABLESPOON OLIVE OIL

½ LB. SHIITAKE MUSHROOMS, STEMMED AND SLICED

1 TABLESPOON SOY SAUCE

1 TEASPOON SESAME OIL

DIRECTIONS

1. Bring salted water to a boil in a medium saucepan and prepare an ice water bath. Add the green beans and boil for 2 minutes. Remove with a slotted spoon and transfer to the ice water bath. When they have cooled completely, drain and set aside.

2. Place the oil in large skillet and warm over medium-high heat. When the oil starts to shimmer, add the mushrooms and sauté until they begin to brown, about 10 minutes. Add the blanched green beans and sauté until they are slightly brown, about 5 minutes. Remove from heat, add the soy sauce, and toss to coat.

3. When the green beans and mushrooms have cooled slightly, add the sesame oil, toss to coat, and serve.

Okra & Tomatoes with Cajun Seasoning

YIELD: **4 SERVINGS**

ACTIVE TIME: **15 MINUTES**

TOTAL TIME: **30 MINUTES**

If you can't find Cajun seasoning, smoked paprika or cumin are good substitutes.

INGREDIENTS

OLIVE OIL, AS NEEDED

1 ONION, CHOPPED

1 LB. OKRA, RINSED WELL AND CHOPPED

1 GARLIC CLOVE, CHOPPED

2 TOMATOES, CHOPPED

1 TEASPOON CAJUN SEASONING

SALT, TO TASTE

DIRECTIONS

1. Place the oil in a 10-inch skillet and warm over medium heat. When the oil starts to shimmer, add the onion and sauté until it starts to brown, about 10 minutes. Add the okra and cook, stirring continuously, until it starts to brown, about 5 minutes.

2. Add the garlic and cook for 1 minute. Add the tomatoes and Cajun seasoning and stir to incorporate. Cook until the tomatoes have completely collapsed and the okra is tender, about 8 minutes. Season with salt and serve immediately.

Potato & Parsnip Latkes

YIELD: **4 SERVINGS**

ACTIVE TIME: **40 MINUTES**

TOTAL TIME: **1 HOUR**

The parsnips improve the traditional latke tremendously, as they add sweetness as well as a nice, crispy texture.

INGREDIENTS

2 RUSSET POTATOES, PEELED AND GRATED

3 PARSNIPS, PEELED, TRIMMED, CORED, AND GRATED

1 TABLESPOON ALL-PURPOSE FLOUR

1 EGG

SALT AND PEPPER, TO TASTE

1 TABLESPOON OLIVE OIL

SOUR CREAM, FOR SERVING

APPLESAUCE, FOR SERVING

DIRECTIONS

1. Preheat the oven to 350°F. Place the grated potatoes in a colander and squeeze one handful at a time until no more liquid can be removed from them. Transfer to a bowl.

2. Add the parsnips, flour, and egg to the potatoes, stir to combine, and season with salt and pepper.

3. Place the oil in a large skillet and warm over medium-high heat. When the oil starts to shimmer, add spoonfuls of the latke mixture to the pan and gently press down until they flatten into patties. Reduce heat to medium-low and cook until brown on both sides, about 8 to 10 minutes per side.

4. When both sides are perfectly brown, test the latkes to see if the interior is fully cooked. If not, place them on a baking sheet and bake in the oven for an additional 10 minutes. Let the cooked latkes cool briefly and then serve with the sour cream and applesauce.

Turnip & Sweet Potato Pommes Anna

If you can pull this dish off, the alternating orange and white discs make for a beautiful presentation.

YIELD: **4 SERVINGS**

ACTIVE TIME: **35 MINUTES**

TOTAL TIME: **50 MINUTES**

INGREDIENTS

3 TABLESPOONS UNSALTED BUTTER

1 LB. SWEET POTATOES, PEELED AND SLICED THIN

1 LB. PURPLE-TOP TURNIPS, PEELED AND SLICED THIN

1 TEASPOON FINELY CHOPPED FRESH THYME

SALT, TO TASTE

DIRECTIONS

1. Warm a 10- to 12-inch skillet over medium heat. Melt 1 tablespoon of the butter and remove the pan from heat. Place one slice of sweet potato along the edge of the pan, followed by a turnip slice. Continue along the edge, alternating slices of sweet potato and turnip. When the outside edge is complete, make another row in the inner circle and then in the very center.

2. Sprinkle with half of the thyme and a pinch of salt. Make another layer with the remaining sweet potato, turnip, thyme, and salt.

3. Dot the top with another tablespoon of butter, place the pan on the stove, and cook over low heat for 5 minutes. Cover the pan with a lid and continue to cook.

4. Remove the lid every 5 minutes to let out steam. Check on the bottom layer after roughly 20 minutes by gently lifting with a spatula. If it isn't browning, remove the lid and continue cooking. If nice and brown, find a plate with flat edges that is the same size as your pan. With one hand on the pan's handle and another on the plate, invert the vegetables onto the plate, then gently slide the veggies back into the pan, browned-side up.

5. Add the remaining butter if the pan seems dry. Cook until tender all the way through, about 10 minutes. To serve, either invert onto a serving plate or, if it holds together in one piece, lift it out with a spatula.

Two Peas in a Pod & Radishes with Mint

YIELD: **4 SERVINGS**

ACTIVE TIME: **15 MINUTES**

TOTAL TIME: **20 MINUTES**

Red radishes turn a lovely rose pink when cooked, which provides lovely contrast with the bright green peas.

INGREDIENTS

1 TABLESPOON OLIVE OIL, PLUS MORE TO TASTE

8 RED RADISHES, QUARTERED

½ LB. SUGAR SNAP PEAS (OR SNOW PEAS)

¼ CUP FROZEN PEAS

1 TABLESPOON FINELY CHOPPED FRESH MINT

SALT, TO TASTE

FRESH LEMON JUICE, TO TASTE

DIRECTIONS

1. Place the oil in a large skillet and warm over medium heat. When the oil starts to shimmer, add the radishes and sauté, stirring occasionally, until they are brown on both of the cut sides, about 10 minutes.

2. Add the sugar snap peas and frozen peas and cook until the frozen peas are heated through and the sugar snaps are just tender, about 3 minutes. Transfer to a bowl and add the mint. Toss to combine, season with salt, lemon juice, and more olive oil, and serve.

Roasted Acorn Squash with Maple Syrup, Butter & Cardamom

YIELD: **2 SERVINGS**

ACTIVE TIME: **15 MINUTES**

TOTAL TIME: **40 MINUTES**

Cardamom is a warm, floral spice that pairs beautifully with maple syrup. The earthy sweetness of acorn squash brings out the best of both.

INGREDIENTS

1 ACORN SQUASH, HALVED AND SEEDED

1 TABLESPOON UNSALTED BUTTER

2 TABLESPOONS REAL MAPLE SYRUP

½ TEASPOON GROUND CARDAMOM

SALT, TO TASTE

2 TABLESPOONS SHELLED AND CHOPPED PISTACHIOS

DIRECTIONS

1. Preheat the oven to 400°F. Cut the bottom of the squash so that it can rest flat when cut-side up. Place the squash on a baking sheet, cut-side down, and roast for 20 minutes. Flip the squash over and place half of the butter on each half. Baste the flesh with the butter, return the baking sheet to the oven, and roast for another 10 minutes.

2. Remove from the oven and divide the maple syrup and ground cardamom between the halves. Season with salt, baste the flesh, return the pan to the oven, and roast for another 10 minutes. Remove from the oven, sprinkle the pistachios over each half, and serve.

Kohlrabi Slaw with Miso Dressing

YIELD: **4 SERVINGS**

ACTIVE TIME: **10 MINUTES**

TOTAL TIME: **10 MINUTES**

The Asian-inflected flavors in this coleslaw are just perfect beside BBQ tempeh or seitan. If you have a mandoline, it will make quick work of slicing the vegetables.

INGREDIENTS

FOR THE DRESSING

1 TABLESPOON WHITE MISO PASTE

1 TABLESPOON RICE VINEGAR

1 TEASPOON SESAME OIL

1 TEASPOON MINCED GINGER

1 TEASPOON SOY SAUCE

3 TABLESPOONS PEANUT OIL

1 TABLESPOON SESAME SEEDS

1 TEASPOON REAL MAPLE SYRUP

FOR THE COLESLAW

3 KOHLRABIES, PEELED AND JULIENNED

2 CARROTS, PEELED AND JULIENNED

2 SHALLOTS, PEELED AND JULIENNED

¼ CUP FINELY CHOPPED FRESH CILANTRO

¼ CUP SHELLED PISTACHIOS, CRUSHED

DIRECTIONS

1. To prepare the dressing, place all of the ingredients in a mixing bowl and stir to combine. Set aside.

2. To begin preparations for the coleslaw, place the kohlrabies, carrots, shallots, and cilantro in a salad bowl and stir to combine.

3. Drizzle a few spoonfuls of the dressing over the coleslaw and stir until evenly coated. Taste, add more dressing if desired, top with the pistachios, and serve.

Hasselback Sweet Potatoes with Lime & Cilantro

YIELD: **4 SERVINGS**

ACTIVE TIME: **15 MINUTES**

TOTAL TIME: **1 HOUR**

A recipe inspired by the great Alice Waters and her classic, **Chez Panisse Vegetables.**

INGREDIENTS

4 SWEET POTATOES

6 TABLESPOONS UNSALTED BUTTER, AT ROOM TEMPERATURE

1 LIME, QUARTERED

¼ CUP FINELY CHOPPED FRESH CILANTRO

DIRECTIONS

1. Preheat the oven to 450°F. While taking care not to cut through the last ¼ inch, cut the sweet potatoes into thin slices. Place the potatoes on a baking sheet, spread the butter over them, and place them in the oven. Roast until fork-tender, 30 to 40 minutes.

2. Remove from the oven, squeeze a wedge of lime over each potato, sprinkle the cilantro on top, and serve.

Succotash

YIELD: **4 SERVINGS**

ACTIVE TIME: **20 MINUTES**

TOTAL TIME: **35 MINUTES**

Switching out the divisive lima bean for protein-rich edamame will make this a welcome sight on any table.

INGREDIENTS

1 LB. MUSHROOMS, STEMMED AND SLICED

1 RED ONION, MINCED

4 CUPS CORN KERNELS

1 RED BELL PEPPER, STEMMED, SEEDED, AND CHOPPED

2 CUPS EDAMAME

½ LB. OKRA, RINSED WELL AND CHOPPED

1 TABLESPOON UNSALTED BUTTER

SALT AND PEPPER, TO TASTE

1 TABLESPOON FINELY CHOPPED FRESH MARJORAM

½ CUP FINELY CHOPPED FRESH BASIL

DIRECTIONS

1. Place a large cast-iron skillet over medium heat, add the mushrooms and cook until they release their liquid and start to brown, about 10 minutes. Reduce heat to low and cook until the mushrooms are a deep brown, about 15 minutes.

2. Add the onion, raise the heat to medium-high, and cook until it starts to soften, about 5 minutes. Add the corn, bell pepper, edamame, and okra and cook, while stirring often, until the corn is tender and bright yellow, about 4 minutes.

3. Add the butter and stir until it has melted and coated all of the vegetables. Season with salt and pepper, add the marjoram and basil, stir to incorporate, and serve.

CHAPTER 6

ENTREES

The age-old argument that vegetarian cuisine cannot produce dishes that are as flavorful, filling, and exciting as those available to the omnivore has always started to gain momentum when it turns to the main course. Luckily, you can now put that debate to rest, and let these dishes do all the talking for you.

In order to quiet the age-old assumptions, we traipse across the globe to uncover gems such as a Spiced Buttermilk Stew with Spinach Dumplings (see page 235) that leans heavily on the philosophy of Indian cuisine, a roasted squash that brilliantly deploys Jamaica's famed jerk marinade (see page 246), and a Chinese-inspired, pan-fried seitan dish (see page 263) that will have everyone begging you for the recipe.

Mushroom & Chard Shepherd's Pie

YIELD: **4 TO 6 SERVINGS**

ACTIVE TIME: **45 MINUTES**

TOTAL TIME: **1 HOUR AND 30 MINUTES**

The substantial savory qualities of chard and mushrooms makes this humble pie feel richer on the palate than the stomach.

INGREDIENTS

6 RUSSET POTATOES, PEELED AND CHOPPED

½ TEASPOON KOSHER SALT, PLUS MORE TO TASTE

11 TABLESPOONS UNSALTED BUTTER, DIVIDED INTO INDIVIDUAL TABLESPOONS

½ CUP MILK

¼ CUP PLAIN YOGURT

BLACK PEPPER, TO TASTE

1 SMALL ONION, MINCED

3 CUPS CHOPPED MUSHROOMS

1 BUNCH SWISS CHARD, WASHED AND CHOPPED

1 TABLESPOON VEGAN WORCESTERSHIRE SAUCE (SEE PAGE 31)

OLIVE OIL, AS NEEDED

DIRECTIONS

1. Preheat the oven to 350°F. Place the potatoes in a large saucepan and cover with cold water. Add the salt. Bring the water to a boil, reduce to a simmer, and cook the potatoes until fork-tender, about 20 minutes.

2. Drain the potatoes and place them in a large bowl. Add 6 tablespoons of the butter, the milk, and the yogurt and mash the potatoes until they are smooth and creamy. Season with salt and pepper and set aside.

3. In a 12-inch cast-iron skillet, melt 3 tablespoons of the butter over medium heat. Add the onion and cook until translucent, about 3 minutes. Add the mushrooms, the chopped stems of the chard (not the leaves), and the Vegan Worcestershire Sauce. Cook for about 3 minutes, while stirring frequently, then reduce the heat to low and continue cooking until the mushrooms and chard stems are soft, another 5 minutes. If the pan seems dry, add a tablespoon of olive oil.

4. Increase the heat to medium and add the chard leaves. Cook, while stirring constantly, until the leaves wilt, about 3 minutes. Remove the skillet from heat and season with salt and pepper.

5. Spread the mashed potatoes over the mixture, distributing the potatoes evenly and smoothing the top with a rubber spatula. Cut the remaining 2 tablespoons of butter into slivers and dot the potatoes with them.

6. Cover with foil and bake for 25 minutes. Remove the foil and bake for another 10 minutes, until the topping is just browned and the filling is bubbly. Remove and briefly let cool before serving.

YIELD: **6 TO 8 SERVINGS**

ACTIVE TIME: **15 MINUTES**

TOTAL TIME: **30 MINUTES**

Spiced Buttermilk Stew with Spinach Dumplings

Like many Indian-inspired recipes, there are a lot of ingredients, but don't be daunted—the final result is well worth it.

INGREDIENTS

FOR THE STEW

8 CUPS BUTTERMILK

½ CUP CHICKPEA FLOUR

1 TABLESPOON TURMERIC

1 TEASPOON KOSHER SALT

1 TABLESPOON OLIVE OIL

1 TEASPOON CORIANDER SEEDS

1 TABLESPOON BLACK MUSTARD SEEDS

2 LARGE YELLOW ONIONS, SLICED INTO THIN HALF-MOONS

6 GARLIC CLOVES, MINCED

2-INCH PIECE FRESH GINGER, PEELED AND MINCED

1 TEASPOON AMCHOOR POWDER

2 SERRANO PEPPERS, SEEDED AND MINCED

FOR THE DUMPLINGS

2 CUPS SPINACH, BLANCHED AND CHOPPED

2 SERRANO PEPPERS, STEMMED, SEEDED, AND MINCED (OPTIONAL)

2 TEASPOONS KOSHER SALT

1 TEASPOON RED PEPPER FLAKES

1½ TEASPOONS CHAAT MASALA

1 CUP CHICKPEA FLOUR

DIRECTIONS

1. To begin preparations for the stew, place half of the buttermilk, the chickpea flour, turmeric, and salt in a blender and puree until smooth. Set the mixture aside.

2. Place the oil in a Dutch oven and warm over high heat. When the oil is shimmering, add the coriander and mustard seeds and cook, while stirring, until they start to pop, about 2 minutes.

3. Reduce the heat to medium and add the onions, garlic, ginger, amchoor powder, and peppers. Sauté until slightly browned and then pour in the buttermilk mixture. Add the remaining buttermilk, reduce the heat so that the stew gently simmers, and prepare the dumplings.

4. To prepare the dumplings, place the spinach, serrano peppers (if using), salt, red pepper flakes, and chaat masala in a mixing bowl and stir to combine. Add the chickpea flour and stir to incorporate. The dough should be quite stiff.

5. Add tablespoons of the dough to the stew. When all of the dumplings have been added, cover the Dutch oven and simmer over low heat until the dumplings are cooked through, about 10 minutes. Ladle into warmed bowls and serve.

NOTE: Amchoor is a sour powder made from the dried flesh of an unripe mango. Crucial to North Indian cuisine, you can find it at better grocery stores or online.

Spinach & Mushroom Quinoa

YIELD: **6 SERVINGS**

ACTIVE TIME: **20 MINUTES**

TOTAL TIME: **5 HOURS**

Folding in the herbs at the end of your preparation packs this dish with tons of fresh flavor.

INGREDIENTS

1½ CUPS QUINOA, RINSED

2½ CUPS VEGETABLE STOCK (SEE PAGE 12)

1 YELLOW ONION, CHOPPED

½ RED BELL PEPPER, STEMMED, SEEDED, AND CHOPPED

¾ LB. PORTOBELLO MUSHROOMS, CHOPPED

2 GARLIC CLOVES, MINCED

1 TABLESPOON KOSHER SALT, PLUS MORE TO TASTE

1 TABLESPOON BLACK PEPPER, PLUS MORE TO TASTE

3 CUPS BABY SPINACH

1½ CUPS FRESH BASIL LEAVES, FINELY CHOPPED

¼ CUP FINELY CHOPPED FRESH DILL

2 TABLESPOONS FINELY CHOPPED FRESH THYME

DIRECTIONS

1. Place all of the ingredients, except for the spinach and fresh herbs, in a slow cooker and cook on high until the quinoa is slightly fluffy, about 4 hours.

2. Add the spinach and turn off the heat. Keep the slow cooker covered and let sit for 1 hour.

3. Fluff the quinoa with a fork, add the basil, dill, and thyme, and fold to incorporate. Season with salt and pepper and serve.

Veggie Burgers

YIELD: **4 SERVINGS**

ACTIVE TIME: **15 MINUTES**

TOTAL TIME: **45 MINUTES**

Every vegetarian chef worth their salt needs a foolproof veggie burger recipe such as this.

INGREDIENTS

1 (14 OZ.) CAN BLACK BEANS, DRAINED AND RINSED

⅓ CUP MINCED SCALLIONS

¼ CUP CHOPPED ROASTED RED PEPPERS

¼ CUP CORN KERNELS

½ CUP PANKO BREAD CRUMBS

1 EGG, LIGHTLY BEATEN

2 TABLESPOONS FINELY CHOPPED FRESH CILANTRO

½ TEASPOON CUMIN

½ TEASPOON CAYENNE PEPPER

½ TEASPOON BLACK PEPPER

1 TEASPOON FRESH LIME JUICE

1 TABLESPOON OLIVE OIL

HAMBURGER BUNS, FOR SERVING

GUACAMOLE (SEE PAGE 36) OR SLICED AVOCADO, FOR SERVING

DIRECTIONS

1. Place half of the beans, the scallions, and roasted red peppers in a food processor and pulse until the mixture is a thick paste. Transfer to a large bowl.

2. Add the corn, bread crumbs, egg, cilantro, cumin, cayenne, black pepper, and lime juice to the bowl and stir to combine. Add the remaining beans and stir until the mixture holds together. Cover the bowl with plastic wrap and let it sit at room temperature for 30 minutes.

3. Place a 12-inch cast-iron skillet over medium-high heat and coat the bottom with the olive oil. Form the mixture into four patties. When the oil starts to shimmer, add the patties, cover the skillet, and cook until browned and cooked through, about 5 minutes per side. Serve immediately on hamburger buns with the Guacamole or sliced avocado.

Mac & Cheese with Browned Butter Bread Crumbs

YIELD: **6 SERVINGS**

ACTIVE TIME: **15 MINUTES**

TOTAL TIME: **1 HOUR**

Even though the cheese in this dish will stick to your ribs, seconds are a must. Reserve it for those nights when you're especially hungry and can afford to relax after the meal.

INGREDIENTS

SALT, TO TASTE

1 LB. ELBOW MACARONI

7 TABLESPOONS UNSALTED BUTTER

2 CUPS PANKO BREAD CRUMBS

½ YELLOW ONION, MINCED

3 TABLESPOONS ALL-PURPOSE FLOUR

1 TABLESPOON YELLOW MUSTARD

1 TEASPOON TURMERIC

1 TEASPOON GRANULATED GARLIC

1 TEASPOON WHITE PEPPER

2 CUPS LIGHT CREAM

2 CUPS WHOLE MILK

1 LB. AMERICAN CHEESE, SLICED

10 OZ. BOURSIN CHEESE

½ LB. EXTRA-SHARP CHEDDAR CHEESE, SLICED

DIRECTIONS

1. Preheat the oven to 400°F. Fill a Dutch oven with water, add salt to taste, and bring to a boil. Add the macaroni and cook until it is just shy of al dente, about 7 minutes. Drain and set aside.

2. Place the pot over medium heat and add 3 tablespoons of the butter. Cook until the butter starts to give off a nutty smell and brown. Add the bread crumbs, stir, and cook for 4 to 5 minutes, until the bread crumbs start to look like wet sand. Remove from the pan and set aside.

3. Wipe the Dutch oven out, place over medium-high heat, and add the onion and the remaining butter. Cook, while stirring, until the onion is soft, about 10 minutes. Gradually add the flour and stir constantly to prevent lumps from forming. Add the mustard, turmeric, granulated garlic, and white pepper and whisk until combined. Add the light cream and the milk and whisk until incorporated. Reduce heat to medium and bring the mixture to a simmer.

4. Once you start to see small bubbles forming around the outside of the mixture, add the cheeses one at a time, stirring to incorporate before adding the next one. When all of the cheeses have been incorporated and the mixture is smooth, cook until the flour taste is gone, about 10 minutes. Return the macaroni to the pot, stir, and top with the bread crumbs.

5. Place the Dutch oven in the oven and bake until the bread crumbs are crispy, 10 to 15 minutes. Remove from the oven and serve immediately.

INGREDIENTS

1½ CUPS ALL-PURPOSE FLOUR,
PLUS MORE FOR DUSTING

1½ TEASPOONS KOSHER SALT, PLUS
MORE TO TASTE

¾ CUP EGG YOLKS

1 TABLESPOON OLIVE OIL

1 BUNCH ASPARAGUS, TRIMMED
AND CHOPPED

½ LB. SNAP PEAS, TRIMMED AND
CHOPPED

4 TABLESPOONS UNSALTED BUTTER

¼ CUP GRATED PARMESAN CHEESE

½ TEASPOON RED PEPPER FLAKES

Tagliatelle with Asparagus & Peas

YIELD: **4 TO 6 SERVINGS**

ACTIVE TIME: **50 MINUTES**

TOTAL TIME: **1 HOUR AND 30 MINUTES**

Making your own pasta may seem daunting, but it's far simpler than you think, as you'll see after making this preparation.

DIRECTIONS

1. Place the flour and salt in a mixing bowl, stir to combine, and make a well in the center. Pour the egg yolks and olive oil into the well and, starting in the center and gradually working to the outside, incorporate the flour into the well. When all the flour has been incorporated, place the dough on a lightly floured work surface and knead until it is a smooth ball. Cover it in plastic wrap and let rest for at least 30 minutes.

2. Divide the dough into quarters. Use a rolling pin to flatten each quarter to a thickness that can go through the widest setting on a pasta maker.

3. Run the rolled pieces of dough through the pasta maker, adjusting the setting to reduce the thickness with each pass. Roll until you can see your hand through the dough. Cut the sheets into 10-inch-long pieces, dust them with flour, stack them on top of each other, and gently roll them up. Cut the roll into ¼-inch-wide strips, unroll, and place the strips on baking sheets lightly dusted with flour.

4. Bring salted water to a boil in a medium saucepan and also in a large saucepan. Place the asparagus and peas in the medium saucepan and cook for 1 minute. Drain and set aside.

5. Place the pasta in the large saucepan and cook for 3 to 4 minutes while stirring constantly. Drain and reserve ¼ cup of the pasta water.

6. Place the butter in a large skillet and melt over medium heat. Add the pasta and vegetables and toss to combine. Add the reserved pasta water, Parmesan, and red pepper flakes and toss to evenly coat. Season to taste and serve.

NOTE: If you don't have a pasta maker, roll out the dough as thin as it can get on a flour-dusted work surface and then cut it into 10-inch-long and ¼-inch-wide strips.

Squash Risotto with Baby Kale, Toasted Walnuts & Dried Cranberries

YIELD: **6 SERVINGS**

ACTIVE TIME: **35 MINUTES**

TOTAL TIME: **1 HOUR**

Risotto is so much more than a bowl of rice, particularly when you add the famous sweetness of butternut squash, which brings the nutty flavor of Arborio rice to the fore.

INGREDIENTS

1 STICK UNSALTED BUTTER

3 CUPS DICED ONIONS

1 SMALL BUTTERNUT SQUASH, PEELED AND DICED

1 TABLESPOON KOSHER SALT, PLUS 2 TEASPOONS

3 CUPS MILK

5 CUPS VEGETABLE STOCK (SEE PAGE 12)

2 CUPS ARBORIO RICE

2 CUPS WHITE WINE

1 TABLESPOON FRESH LEMON JUICE

3 CUPS BABY KALE, STEMMED AND CHOPPED

¾ CUP TOASTED WALNUTS, CHOPPED

½ CUP DRIED CRANBERRIES

DIRECTIONS

1. Place 2 tablespoons of the butter in a saucepan and melt over medium heat. Add half of the onions and cook until translucent. Add the squash, the tablespoon of salt, and the milk, reduce the heat to low, and cook until the squash is tender, about 20 minutes. Strain, discard the cooking liquid, and transfer the squash and onions to a blender. Puree until smooth and then set aside.

2. Place the stock in a saucepan, bring to a boil, and remove from heat.

3. Place the remaining butter in a large skillet with high sides and melt over medium heat. Add the remaining onions and cook until translucent, about 3 minutes. Add the rice and remaining salt and cook, while stirring constantly, until you can smell a toasted nutty aroma. Be careful not to brown the rice.

4. Deglaze the pan with the white wine, add the lemon juice, and continue to stir until all the liquid has been absorbed. Add the stock in 1-cup increments and stir constantly until all of the stock has been absorbed. Add the squash puree and kale, stir to incorporate, and season to taste. Stir in the walnuts and dried cranberries and serve immediately.

JERK MARINADE

Place ¼ cup real maple syrup, ¼ cup lightly packed brown sugar, 1 tablespoon molasses, ½ teaspoon cayenne pepper, 1 teaspoon chili powder, 1 teaspoon paprika, 1 teaspoon cumin, ½ teaspoon ground cloves, 1 teaspoon cinnamon, ½ teaspoon nutmeg, 2 teaspoons kosher salt, 1 teaspoon black pepper, 2 teaspoons minced fresh ginger, 1 tablespoon finely chopped thyme, 2 tablespoons sliced scallions, 2 tablespoons chopped shallot, 1 tablespoon minced garlic, and 1 tablespoon fresh lime juice in a blender and puree until smooth.

Jerk Acorn Squash

Melding the sweet-and-savory taste of the acorn squash and the delicious spice of the jerk marinade is irresistible.

YIELD: **4 SERVINGS**

ACTIVE TIME: **25 MINUTES**

TOTAL TIME: **2 HOURS**

INGREDIENTS

FOR THE SQUASH & SALAD

2 ACORN SQUASH

JERK MARINADE (SEE SIDEBAR)

1 TABLESPOON OLIVE OIL

½ TEASPOON KOSHER SALT

¼ TEASPOON BLACK PEPPER

¼ TEASPOON PAPRIKA

6 CUPS BABY KALE

½ CUP DRIED CRANBERRIES

1 CUP CRUMBLED FETA CHEESE

FOR THE MAPLE VINAIGRETTE

½ CUP APPLE CIDER VINEGAR

½ CUP REAL MAPLE SYRUP

1 TEASPOON ORANGE ZEST

2 TEASPOONS DIJON MUSTARD

1 TABLESPOON KOSHER SALT

1 TEASPOON BLACK PEPPER

2 ICE CUBES

1½ CUPS OLIVE OIL

DIRECTIONS

1. Preheat the oven to 400°F. To begin preparations for the squash and salad, cut the squash in half lengthwise, remove the seeds, and reserve them. Trim the bottom of the squash so that each half can sit flat when cut-side up on a baking sheet. Score the flesh in a crosshatch pattern, cutting approximately ⅛ inch into the flesh. Brush some of the marinade on the squash and then fill the cavities with ⅓ cup. Place the baking sheet in the oven and roast until the squash is tender, about 45 minutes to 1 hour. As the squash is cooking, brush the flesh with the marinade in the cavities every 15 minutes. Remove from the oven and let cool. Lower the oven temperature to 350°F.

2. Rinse the seeds to remove any pulp. Pat the seeds dry, place them in a mixing bowl, and add the olive oil, salt, pepper, and paprika. Toss to combine and then place the seeds on a baking sheet. Place in the oven and bake until they are light brown and crispy, about 7 minutes.

3. Place the toasted seeds, kale, and cranberries in a salad bowl and toss to combine.

4. To prepare the vinaigrette, place all of the ingredients, except for the olive oil, in a blender. Turn on high and add the oil in a slow stream. Puree until the mixture has emulsified.

5. Add the vinaigrette to the salad bowl. Toss to coat evenly and top the salad with the crumbled feta. To serve, place a bed of salad on each plate and place one of the roasted halves of squash on top of each portion.

Ratatouille

YIELD: **4 SERVINGS**

ACTIVE TIME: **40 MINUTES**

TOTAL TIME: **2 HOURS**

Some people think sausage is an essential ingredient in a traditional ratatouille, but when your garden is at its peak, this dish has enough flavor to carry on without it.

INGREDIENTS

⅓ CUP OLIVE OIL

6 GARLIC CLOVES, MINCED

1 EGGPLANT, CHOPPED

2 ZUCCHINI, SLICED INTO HALF-MOONS

2 BELL PEPPERS, STEMMED, SEEDED, AND CHOPPED

4 TOMATOES, SEEDED AND CHOPPED

SALT AND PEPPER, TO TASTE

DIRECTIONS

1. Place a 12-inch cast-iron skillet over medium-high heat and add half of the olive oil. When the oil starts to shimmer, add the garlic and eggplant and cook, while stirring, until pieces are coated with oil and just starting to sizzle, about 2 minutes.

2. Reduce the heat to medium, add the zucchini, peppers, and remaining oil, and stir to combine. Cover the skillet and cook, while stirring occasionally, until the eggplant, zucchini, and peppers are almost tender, about 15 minutes.

3. Add the tomatoes, stir to combine, and cook until the eggplant, zucchini, and peppers are extremely tender and the tomatoes are wilted, about 25 minutes. Remove the skillet from heat, season with salt and pepper, and allow to sit for at least 1 hour. Reheat before serving.

Green Bean & Tofu Casserole

YIELD: **4 SERVINGS**

ACTIVE TIME: **5 MINUTES**

TOTAL TIME: **48 HOURS**

Slow roasting is the key here, as it concentrates everything the tofu soaked up while marinating.

INGREDIENTS

FOR THE MARINADE

3 TABLESPOONS SOY SAUCE

2 TABLESPOONS RICE VINEGAR

1 TABLESPOON SESAME OIL

1 TABLESPOON HONEY

1 PINCH CINNAMON

1 PINCH BLACK PEPPER

FOR THE CASSEROLE

1 LB. EXTRA-FIRM TOFU, DRAINED AND CHOPPED

1 LB. GREEN BEANS

4 OZ. SHIITAKE MUSHROOMS, SLICED

2 TABLESPOONS SESAME OIL

1 TABLESPOON SOY SAUCE

2 TABLESPOONS SESAME SEEDS, FOR GARNISH

DIRECTIONS

1. To prepare the marinade, place all of the ingredients in a small bowl and stir to combine.

2. To begin preparations for the casserole, place the marinade and the tofu in a resealable plastic bag, place it in the refrigerator, and let marinate for 2 days.

3. Preheat the oven to 375°F. Remove the cubes of tofu from the bag. Place the green beans, mushrooms, sesame oil, and soy sauce in the bag and shake until the vegetables are coated.

4. Line a 9 x 13-inch baking pan with parchment paper and place the tofu on it in an even layer. Place in the oven and roast for 35 minutes. Remove the pan, flip the cubes of tofu over, and push them to the edge of the pan. Add the green bean-and-mushroom mixture, return the pan to the oven, and roast for 15 minutes, or until the green beans are cooked to your preference. Remove the pan from the oven, garnish with the sesame seeds, and serve.

Sweet & Spicy Roasted Barley

YIELD: 4 SERVINGS

ACTIVE TIME: 20 MINUTES

TOTAL TIME: 1 HOUR AND 50 MINUTES

This dish is light, sweet, spicy, and nutty. Considering how affordable all of the ingredients are, that's whole a lot of flavor for not very much money.

INGREDIENTS

5 CARROTS, PEELED AND CUT INTO 3-INCH PIECES

OLIVE OIL, TO TASTE

SALT AND PEPPER, TO TASTE

6 DRIED PASILLA PEPPERS

2¼ CUPS BOILING WATER

1 CUP PEARL BARLEY

1 RED ONION, MINCED

2 TABLESPOONS ADOBO SEASONING

1 TABLESPOON SUGAR

1 TABLESPOON CHILI POWDER

¼ CUP FINELY CHOPPED FRESH OREGANO

DIRECTIONS

1. Preheat the oven to 375°F. Place the carrots in a 9 x 13-inch baking pan, drizzle the olive oil over them, and season with salt and pepper. Place in the oven and roast until the carrots are slightly soft to the touch, about 45 minutes.

2. While the carrots are cooking, open the Pasilla peppers and discard the seeds and stems. Place the peppers in a bowl, add the boiling water, and cover the bowl with aluminum foil.

3. When the carrots are cooked, remove the pan from the oven and add the remaining ingredients and the liquid the peppers have been soaking in. Chop the reconstituted peppers, add them to the pan, and spread the mixture so that the liquid is covering the barley. Cover the pan tightly with aluminum foil, place it in the oven, and bake until the barley is tender, about 45 minutes. Fluff with a fork and serve immediately.

INGREDIENTS

FOR THE SALAD

¾ LB. BEAN SPROUTS

1 TABLESPOON BLACK SESAME
SEEDS

2 SCALLIONS, TRIMMED AND
SLICED THIN

2 TABLESPOONS SESAME OIL

2 TEASPOONS SOY SAUCE

⅛ TEASPOON RED PEPPER FLAKES

PINCH OF GROUND GINGER

ZEST OF 1 ORANGE

FOR THE RAMEN

¼ CUP SESAME SEEDS

WATER, AS NEEDED

2 TABLESPOONS SESAME OIL

4 GARLIC CLOVES, MINCED

2-INCH PIECE FRESH GINGER,
PEELED AND MINCED

2 SHALLOTS, MINCED

2 TEASPOONS CHILI GARLIC SAUCE

6 TABLESPOONS WHITE MISO
PASTE

2 TABLESPOONS SUGAR

2 TABLESPOONS SAKE

8 CUPS VEGETABLE STOCK (SEE
PAGE 12)

SALT AND PEPPER, TO TASTE

NOODLES FROM 2 PACKETS RAMEN

Miso Ramen with Spicy Bean Sprout Salad

YIELD: **4 SERVINGS**

ACTIVE TIME: **20 MINUTES**

TOTAL TIME: **45 MINUTES**

The constantly shifting flavor of miso and a refreshing bean sprout salad sever any connections to the dreaded college standby.

DIRECTIONS

1. To prepare the salad, bring water to a boil in a small saucepan. Add the bean sprouts and cook for 2 minutes. Drain and let cool. Place the remaining ingredients in a salad bowl and stir to combine. Add the cooled bean sprouts, gently stir to incorporate, and set aside.

2. To begin preparations for the ramen, place the sesame seeds in a dry skillet and toast over medium heat until browned, about 2 minutes. Remove from the pan and use a mortar and pestle to grind them into a paste, adding water as needed.

3. Place the sesame oil in a large saucepan and warm over medium heat. When the oil starts to shimmer, add the garlic, ginger, and shallots and cook until fragrant, about 2 minutes.

4. Raise the heat to medium-high and add the chili garlic sauce, miso, toasted sesame paste, sugar, sake, and stock and stir to combine. Bring to a boil, reduce heat so that the soup simmers, and season with salt and pepper. Simmer for about 5 minutes and remove from heat.

5. While the soup is simmering, cook the noodles according to manufacturer's instructions. Drain the noodles and place them in warmed bowls. Pour the soup over the noodles and top each portion with the bean sprout salad.

NOTE: If you're looking to add a little bit more substance to this ramen, top each portion with a poached egg.

Soba Noodles with Marinated Eggplant & Tofu

YIELD: **4 SERVINGS**

ACTIVE TIME: **45 MINUTES**

TOTAL TIME: **1 HOUR AND 45 MINUTES**

An easy meal that combines eggplant with its best companions: ginger, soy, and sesame oil.

INGREDIENTS

FOR THE MARINADE

2 TABLESPOONS RICE VINEGAR

3 TABLESPOONS SOY SAUCE

1 TABLESPOON TOASTED SESAME OIL

½ TEASPOON SUGAR

2 GARLIC CLOVES, MINCED

FOR THE DRESSING

1 TABLESPOON RICE VINEGAR

1 TABLESPOON PEANUT OIL

1 TEASPOON SOY SAUCE

1 TABLESPOON TOASTED SESAME OIL

1-INCH PIECE FRESH GINGER, PEELED AND GRATED

FOR THE NOODLES

3 EGGPLANTS (ABOUT 2 LBS.)

½ LB. SOBA NOODLES

Continued...

DIRECTIONS

1. To prepare the marinade, place all of the ingredients in a small bowl and stir to combine. To prepare the dressing, place all of the ingredients in a separate small bowl and stir to combine. Set the marinade and the dressing aside.

2. To begin preparations for the noodles, trim both ends of the eggplants, slice the eggplants in half, and cut them into ½-inch pieces. Place in a mixing bowl, add the marinade, and toss to combine. Let stand for 1 hour at room temperature.

3. Bring a large pot of water to a boil. Add the noodles and stir for the first minute to prevent any sticking. Cook until tender but still chewy, 5 to 7 minutes. Drain, rinse under cold water, drain again, and place in a large bowl. Add the dressing, toss to coat, and set aside.

4. Warm a wok or a large skillet over medium heat for 2 to 3 minutes. Raise heat to medium-high and add 2 tablespoons of the peanut oil. When it begins to shimmer, add the eggplant cubes and a couple pinches of salt and stir-fry until the eggplant softens and turn golden, 5 to 6 minutes. Using a slotted spoon, transfer the eggplant to a paper towel–lined plate. Add the remaining peanut oil and the tofu cubes to the pan and stir-fry until they turn golden all over, 4 to 5 minutes. Using a slotted spoon, transfer the tofu to a separate paper towel–lined plate.

Continued...

3 TABLESPOONS PEANUT OIL

SALT, TO TASTE

¾ LB. EXTRA-FIRM TOFU, DRAINED AND DICED

6 SCALLIONS, TRIMMED AND CHOPPED, FOR GARNISH

5. Divide the soba noodles between four bowls. Arrange the eggplant and tofu on top and garnish with the scallions.

BÉCHAMEL SAUCE

Place 2 tablespoons unsalted butter in a saucepan and melt it over low heat. Add 2 tablespoons flour, whisk to combine, and cook for 1 minute. Gradually add 1 cup milk, whisking constantly to prevent lumps from forming. Continue whisking until the sauce has thickened, about 5 minutes. Add salt and pepper to taste and a pinch of ground nutmeg, stir to incorporate, and serve.

INGREDIENTS

1 CUP DRY RED WINE

2 TABLESPOONS UNSALTED BUTTER

3 SHALLOTS, MINCED

SALT AND PEPPER, TO TASTE

2 GARLIC CLOVES, PEELED AND MINCED

1 LB. CREMINI MUSHROOMS, STEMMED AND SLICED THIN

1 OZ. DRIED PORCINI MUSHROOMS, RECONSTITUTED AND CHOPPED, SOAKING LIQUID RESERVED

2 TABLESPOONS FINELY CHOPPED FRESH THYME, PLUS MORE FOR GARNISH

BÉCHAMEL SAUCE (SEE SIDEBAR)

½ LB. DRIED LASAGNA NOODLES

1½ CUPS GRATED PARMESAN CHEESE

Porcini Mushroom & Béchamel Lasagna

YIELD: **6 SERVINGS**

ACTIVE TIME: **1 HOUR**

TOTAL TIME: **2 HOURS**

Bewitching and earthy porcini mushrooms and citrusy, minty thyme pool their considerable talents to make this lasagna well worth the time invested.

DIRECTIONS

1. Place the wine in a small saucepan and bring to a boil. Cook until it has reduced almost by half, about 5 minutes. Remove from heat and set aside.

2. Warm a large, deep skillet over medium heat for 2 to 3 minutes and then add the butter. When the butter has melted, add the shallots and a pinch of salt and stir. Once the shallots begin to gently sizzle, reduce the temperature to low, cover the pan, and cook, stirring occasionally, until they are soft, about 10 minutes. Stir in the garlic and cook for 30 seconds.

3. Raise the heat to medium-high, add the cremini and porcini mushrooms and the thyme, season with salt, and stir. Cook, while stirring frequently, until the mushrooms begin to release their liquid, about 5 minutes. Add the reduced wine, the porcini soaking liquid, and a pinch of salt and bring to a gentle simmer. Cook, while stirring occasionally, until the mushrooms are tender and the liquid has reduced by half, 12 to 15 minutes. Remove from the heat, season to taste, and then stir in the Béchamel Sauce.

4. Preheat the oven to 350°F. Bring a large pot of water to a boil. Once it's boiling, add salt (1 tablespoon for every 4 cups water) and stir. Add the lasagna sheets and cook until just slightly tender, about 5 minutes. Transfer the cooked sheets to a large bowl of cold water, allow them to cool completely, then arrange them in a single layer on kitchen towels.

5. Cover the bottom of a deep 9 x 13-inch baking pan with some of the mushroom mixture. Cover with a layer of noodles, making sure they are slightly overlapping. Cover with a layer of the mushroom mixture and sprinkle ½ cup of the Parmesan on top. Repeat this layering two more times, ending with a layer of the mushroom mixture topped with the remaining Parmesan. Cover the pan loosely with aluminum foil, place in the oven, and bake 35 for minutes. Remove the foil and continue to bake until the edges of the lasagna sheets are lightly browned, about 12 minutes. For nice, clean slices, remove the lasagna from the oven and allow it to rest for at least 20 minutes before slicing.

Thai Fried Rice with Seitan

YIELD: **4 SERVINGS**

ACTIVE TIME: **35 MINUTES**

TOTAL TIME: **1 HOUR**

The directions call for kohlrabi and peas, but you can include any vegetable you like, just cut it into very small cubes to give it equal footing with all the other ingredients and cook each one separately until done.

INGREDIENTS

1 CUP JASMINE RICE

1½ CUPS WATER

2 TABLESPOONS OLIVE OIL, PLUS MORE AS NEEDED

½ LB. SEITAN, RINSED AND DICED

2 TABLESPOONS SOY SAUCE, PLUS MORE TO TASTE

2 TABLESPOONS RICE VINEGAR

1 TABLESPOON SUGAR

1 SHALLOT, DICED

1 KOHLRABI, PEELED AND DICED

1-INCH PIECE FRESH GINGER, PEELED AND MINCED

½ CUP FROZEN PEAS

½ CUP DICED PINEAPPLE

¼ CUP CASHEWS

¼ CUP FINELY CHOPPED FRESH CILANTRO, FOR GARNISH

LIME WEDGES, FOR SERVING

DIRECTIONS

1. Place the rice and water in a saucepan and simmer for 20 minutes. Remove from heat, fluff with a fork, and let cool, uncovered, so that it dries out a little. Set aside.

2. Place 1 tablespoon of the oil in a large skillet and warm over high heat. When the oil starts to shimmer, add the seitan and sauté until it starts to brown, about 3 minutes.

3. Place the soy sauce, 1 tablespoon of the vinegar, and the sugar in a small bowl and stir to combine. Pour this mixture over the seitan and cook until the liquid has reduced to a glaze. Transfer the seitan to a bowl and set aside.

4. Place the remaining ingredients in a larger skillet and warm over high heat. When the oil is shimmering, add the shallot and kohlrabi. Sauté until brown, about 8 minutes, and then transfer to the bowl containing the seitan.

5. Add the ginger and the remaining oil to the pan. Sauté for 2 minutes and then add the rice. It is very likely that the rice will stick to the bottom of the pan. Do your best to scrape it off with a spatula. Cook the rice until it starts to brown, about 5 to 10 minutes, taking care not to let it become too mushy. Season with soy sauce, add the remaining rice vinegar, and stir to incorporate.

6. Add the pineapple, cashews, kohlrabi, shallot, frozen peas, and seitan to the pan. Gently fold to incorporate and cook for another minute to heat everything through. Season to taste, garnish with the cilantro, and serve with the lime wedges.

INGREDIENTS

FOR THE SAUCE

½ CUP WATER, PLUS MORE AS NEEDED

⅓ CUP SUGAR

¼ CUP MUSHROOM SOY SAUCE

½ CUP SOY SAUCE

¼ CUP WHITE WINE VINEGAR

2 GARLIC CLOVES, MINCED

1-INCH PIECE FRESH GINGER, PEELED AND MINCED

FOR THE BUDDHA SEITAN

1 LB. SEITAN

⅓ CUP VEGETABLE OIL, PLUS MORE AS NEEDED

⅓ CUP CORNSTARCH

½ LB. MUSHROOMS, STEMMED AND QUARTERED

1 SHALLOT, MINCED

½ LB. YU CHOY OR BABY BOK CHOY

SESAME SEEDS, FOR GARNISH

JASMINE RICE, COOKED, FOR SERVING

Buddha Seitan

YIELD: **4 TO 6 SERVINGS**

ACTIVE TIME: **35 MINUTES**

TOTAL TIME: **45 MINUTES**

If you're not a fan of seitan, substitute eggplant or your favorite vegetables—the sauce is so good that a delightful dinner is guaranteed.

DIRECTIONS

1. To prepare the sauce, place all of the ingredients in a bowl and whisk to combine. Set the sauce aside.

2. To begin preparations for the Buddha seitan, rinse the seitan to remove any broth and tear it into bite-sized pieces. Pat the seitan dry with paper towels. Place the oil in a small bowl and gradually add the cornstarch, while stirring constantly to prevent lumps from forming.

3. Add vegetable oil to a Dutch oven until it is about 3 inches deep. Heat to 350°F or until a pea-sized bit of seitan dropped in the oil sizzles on contact. Dredge the pieces of seitan in the cornstarch mixture until completely coated. Working in batches, gently drop the seitan in the oil and fry, turning them so they cook evenly, for about 3 to 5 minutes. Transfer the cooked seitan to a paper towel–lined plate. Do not discard the cornstarch mixture because you will use it to thicken the sauce later on.

4. Place a small amount of oil in a large skillet and warm over medium heat. Add the mushrooms, making sure they are in one layer, and cook until they start to brown, about 10 minutes. Transfer the mushrooms to a bowl, add the shallot to the pan, and sauté until it is fragrant, about 1 minute. Add the yu choy or baby bok choy and cook until it starts to wilt, about 2 minutes. Transfer the mixture to the bowl containing the mushrooms.

5. Pour the sauce into the pan and scrape up any browned bits that have accumulated on the bottom of the pan. Bring to a boil, add a teaspoon of the cornstarch mixture, and stir until the sauce has thickened. If it does not thicken enough, add another teaspoon. If it is too thick, add a little water. When the sauce has reached the desired consistency, return the seitan and vegetables to the pan and toss to coat. Sprinkle the sesame seeds on top and serve over the jasmine rice.

Saag Aloo

YIELD: **4 SERVINGS**

ACTIVE TIME: **15 MINUTES**

TOTAL TIME: **30 MINUTES**

A simple vegetable curry that never disappoints, and always impresses. In other words, a perfect dish for those nights when a friend drops by unexpectedly.

INGREDIENTS

1 TABLESPOON OLIVE OIL

½ LB. FINGERLING OR RED POTATOES, CHOPPED

1 SMALL ONION, CHOPPED

1 TEASPOON MUSTARD SEEDS

1 TEASPOON CUMIN

1 GARLIC CLOVE, CHOPPED

1-INCH PIECE FRESH GINGER, PEELED AND MINCED

1 LB. FROZEN CHOPPED SPINACH

1 TEASPOON RED PEPPER FLAKES

½ CUP WATER

SALT, TO TASTE

2 TABLESPOONS PLAIN YOGURT, OR TO TASTE

DIRECTIONS

1. Place the oil and potatoes in a large skillet and cook over medium heat until the potatoes just start to brown, about 5 minutes.

2. Add the onion, mustard seeds, and cumin and cook until the onion starts to soften about 5 minutes. Add the garlic and ginger and cook, stirring constantly, until fragrant, about 2 minutes.

3. Add the frozen spinach, red pepper flakes, and water and cover the pan with a lid. Cook, stirring occasionally, until the spinach is heated through, about 10 minutes.

4. Remove the cover and cook until all of the liquid has evaporated. Season with salt, add the yogurt, and stir to incorporate. Add more yogurt if you prefer a creamier dish, stir to incorporate, and serve.

INGREDIENTS

FOR THE SPÄTZLE

2 LBS. SWISS CHARD

1½ TABLESPOONS KOSHER SALT, PLUS MORE TO TASTE

4 EXTRA-LARGE EGGS

1 TEASPOON GRATED FRESH NUTMEG

2 CUPS ALL-PURPOSE FLOUR, PLUS MORE AS NEEDED

¼ CUP WATER

MILK, AT ROOM TEMPERATURE, AS NEEDED

OLIVE OIL, FOR DRIZZLING

FOR THE GORGONZOLA CREAM

2 CUPS HEAVY CREAM

4 OZ. GORGONZOLA DOLCE CHEESE, CHOPPED

⅔ CUP GRATED PARMESAN CHEESE

1 TEASPOON GRATED FRESH NUTMEG

SALT AND WHITE PEPPER, TO TASTE

Chard Spätzle with Gorgonzola Cream

YIELD: **6 SERVINGS**

ACTIVE TIME: **1 HOUR**

TOTAL TIME: **2 HOURS**

Spätzle has a consistency somewhere between a pasta and a dumpling. The chard in this recipe gives it a nice herbal note that is perfectly complemented by the Gorgonzola Cream.

DIRECTIONS

1. To begin preparations for the spätzle, remove the stems from the chard and discard. Bring a large pot of salted water to a boil. Add the chard leaves and cook until wilted, about 3 minutes. Using a strainer, transfer the greens to a colander set in a large bowl. Reserve the cooking water to cook the spätzle.

2. Rinse the chard under cold water, drain well, and squeeze the chard to remove as much liquid as possible. Transfer to a clean kitchen towel and pat dry.

3. Place the chard, eggs, 1½ tablespoons salt, and nutmeg in a food processor and pulse until the chard is shredded. Add the flour and water and process until the mixture is smooth, about 3 minutes, stopping to scrape down the work bowl as necessary. Transfer the batter to a medium bowl. At this point, the dough should be more like pancake batter; if it seems too thick, add milk, 1 teaspoon at a time, until the consistency becomes thinner. Cover with plastic wrap and let rest for 1 hour at room temperature.

4. To prepare the gorgonzola cream, place the cream and cheeses in a medium saucepan and cook, stirring occasionally, over medium heat until the sauce is smooth and gently simmering, about 5 minutes. Continue to simmer the sauce until it is thick enough to coat the back of a wooden spoon, 8 to 9 minutes. Stir in the nutmeg, season with salt and white pepper, and set aside.

5. Bring the pot of water you used to cook the greens in back to a boil. Reduce heat so the water gently boils. Grease a spätzle maker with nonstick cooking spray and push handfuls of the dough into the boiling water. Stir the pot from time to time with a long wooden spoon to dislodge any spätzle stuck to the bottom of the pot. Cook until they float to the surface, about 1 minute. Quickly remove them with a strainer and transfer to a parchment-lined baking sheet. Drizzle with olive oil so that they don't stick together and tent loosely with aluminum foil to keep them warm. Repeat until all of the spätzle have been cooked and serve with the gorgonzola cream.

Caribbean-Style Pigeon Peas

YIELD: **4 SERVINGS**

ACTIVE TIME: **30 MINUTES**

TOTAL TIME: **1 HOUR**

If this is not coming out quite to your liking the first few times you make it, tinker with the amount of molasses and brown sugar until it's just right.

INGREDIENTS

2 TABLESPOONS COCONUT OIL

2 TABLESPOONS BROWN SUGAR

2 TEASPOONS MOLASSES, PLUS MORE AS NEEDED

2 CUPS PIGEON PEAS

1 ONION, CHOPPED

2 GARLIC CLOVES, MINCED

2 TO 3 PIMIENTO PEPPERS, CHOPPED

1 TOMATO, CHOPPED

1 CUP PEELED AND CHOPPED PUMPKIN

2 SCALLIONS, TRIMMED AND CHOPPED

1 TEASPOON FINELY CHOPPED FRESH THYME

¼ CUP FINELY CHOPPED FRESH CILANTRO

1 CUP COCONUT MILK

1 CUP WATER

1 WHOLE SCOTCH BONNET PEPPER (OPTIONAL)

SALT AND PEPPER, TO TASTE

DIRECTIONS

1. Place the oil in a Dutch oven and warm over medium heat. When the oil starts to shimmer, add the brown sugar and cook until it is bubbling and starting to smoke, about 3 minutes.

2. Add the molasses and pigeon peas, being careful not to splatter the caramel. Cover and let simmer for a few minutes, stirring and checking on them every so often.

3. Uncover the pot, raise heat to high, and cook, stirring constantly, until a majority of the moisture has evaporated, 1 to 2 minutes.

4. Add the onion, garlic, pimiento peppers, tomato, pumpkin, green onion, thyme, and cilantro and sauté for 1 minute.

5. Add the coconut milk, water, and Scotch bonnet pepper (if using) and stir to combine. Bring to a boil, then reduce the heat so that it simmers. Simmer until the peas are tender and the pumpkin can be mashed easily, 20 to 30 minutes.

6. Season with salt and pepper and ladle into warmed bowls.

Maple Roasted Vegetables with Caramelized Onions & Mashed Potatoes

YIELD: **4 SERVINGS**

ACTIVE TIME: **25 MINUTES**

TOTAL TIME: **1 HOUR**

Balancing the earthiness of the root vegetables with maple syrup and caramelized onions make this a dish you're certain to become sweet on.

INGREDIENTS

1 STICK UNSALTED BUTTER, PLUS MORE FOR SERVING

4 LARGE ONIONS, SLICED

1 RUTABAGA, PEELED AND DICED

1 BUNCH BEETS, PEELED AND DICED

2 LARGE CARROTS, PEELED AND DICED

2 TABLESPOONS OLIVE OIL

3 TABLESPOONS REAL MAPLE SYRUP

SALT AND PEPPER, TO TASTE

1½ LBS. POTATOES, PEELED AND DICED

¾ CUP HEAVY CREAM

DIRECTIONS

1. Preheat the oven to 375°F. Melt 3 tablespoons of the butter in a skillet over medium-high heat and then add the onions. Raise heat to high and cook the onions for 2 minutes. Reduce heat to low and cook, stirring occasionally, until the onions have caramelized, 30 to 40 minutes.

2. While the onions are cooking, place the rutabaga, beets, carrots, olive oil, maple syrup, salt, and pepper in a bowl and toss to combine. Spread evenly in a roasting pan and place the pan in the oven. Roast for 45 minutes, turning the vegetables occasionally until they are browned.

3. As the vegetables roast, place the potatoes in a large saucepan and cover with water. Bring to a boil and cook until tender, about 15 minutes. Drain and immediately transfer to a large mixing bowl. Add 2½ tablespoons of the butter and half of the cream. Use a handheld mixer to slowly combine the ingredients. Once the potatoes are half-mashed, add the remaining butter and cream, season with salt and pepper, and mash until smooth and creamy.

4. To serve, place a dollop of the mashed potatoes on a plate and make a well in the center. Spoon some of the roasted vegetables into the well and top with a spoonful of caramelized onions and additional butter.

Tofu San Bei

YIELD: **4 SERVINGS**

ACTIVE TIME: **30 MINUTES**

TOTAL TIME: **1 HOUR**

San bei means "three cups" in Mandarin, which is a reference to the quantities of soy sauce, sesame oil, and rice wine traditionally used in the sauce. Altering the formula a tad results in this scrumptious dish.

INGREDIENTS

1 LB. EXTRA-FIRM TOFU

3 TABLESPOONS PEANUT OIL

1½ TEASPOONS CORNSTARCH, PLUS MORE AS NEEDED

3 TABLESPOONS TOASTED SESAME OIL

8 GARLIC CLOVES, SMASHED

2-INCH PIECE FRESH GINGER, PEELED AND CHOPPED INTO 8 PIECES

10 SCALLIONS, TRIMMED AND CHOPPED

SALT, TO TASTE

3 TABLESPOONS SUGAR

¾ CUP WATER, PLUS 1 TABLESPOON

¾ CUP SHAOXING RICE WINE

⅓ CUP SOY SAUCE

⅓ LB. RAMEN NOODLES

2 HANDFULS FRESH BASIL LEAVES (THAI BASIL PREFERRED), SLICED THIN, FOR GARNISH

DIRECTIONS

1. Drain the tofu and cut it into ½-inch-wide slices. Arrange them in a single layer on a paper towel–lined tray. Cover with paper towels and pat dry. Let them sit for 30 minutes, changing the paper towels after 15 minutes.

2. Warm a large skillet over medium heat for 3 minutes. Add the peanut oil and warm until it starts to shimmer. Dredge the tofu slices in a shallow dish containing cornstarch and tap to remove any excess. Working in batches, add the tofu in a single layer to the skillet. Raise heat to medium-high and cook until the tofu is browned, 3 to 4 minutes per side. Transfer to a paper towel–lined plate to drain.

3. Wipe out the skillet and add the sesame oil to the pan. Reduce heat to medium and add the smashed garlic, ginger, scallions, and two pinches of salt once the oil starts to shimmer. Cook, stirring frequently, until fragrant, about 2 minutes. Add the sugar and stir until it has melted. Stir in the ¾ cup water, rice wine, and soy sauce, raise heat to medium-high, and bring to a boil. Reduce the heat to low, cover, and simmer, stirring occasionally, for 10 minutes.

4. Place the 1½ teaspoons cornstarch and 1 tablespoon water in a small bowl and stir until the mixture is smooth. Add the slurry to the sauce and stir until thoroughly incorporated.

Continued...

Continue to cook, stirring occasionally, until the sauce thickens slightly, about 5 minutes. Add the tofu slices and cook until warmed through, about 3 minutes.

5. As the sauce simmers, bring a large pot of water to a boil. Add the ramen noodles and stir for the first minute to prevent any sticking. Cook until tender and chewy, drain, and divide the noodles between four warm, shallow bowls. Top with the tofu slices, ladle the sauce over the top, garnish with the basil, and serve.

Butternut Squash Ravioli

YIELD: **6 SERVINGS**

ACTIVE TIME: **45 MINUTES**

TOTAL TIME: **1 HOUR AND 45 MINUTES**

Butternut squash ravioli is ubiquitous at this point, but adding a little gorgonzola to the filling adds enough zing that no one will be able to categorize this dish as old hat.

INGREDIENTS

1 CUP "00" FLOUR, PLUS MORE FOR DUSTING

1 PINCH KOSHER SALT, PLUS MORE TO TASTE

10 EGG YOLKS, BEATEN

1 TEASPOON OLIVE OIL, PLUS MORE AS NEEDED

1 TABLESPOON UNSALTED BUTTER

1½ LBS. BUTTERNUT SQUASH, HALVED LENGTHWISE AND SEEDED

¼ CUP SOFT BREAD CRUMBS

½ CUP GRATED PARMESAN CHEESE, PLUS MORE FOR GARNISH

¼ CUP CRUMBLED GORGONZOLA CHEESE

1 TEASPOON GRATED FRESH NUTMEG

10 FRESH ROSEMARY LEAVES, MINCED

1 EGG, BEATEN

1 TABLESPOON WATER

CREAMY LEEK SAUCE (SEE PAGE 28), FOR SERVING

DIRECTIONS

1. Place the flour and salt in a mixing bowl, stir to combine, and make a well in the center. Place eight of the egg yolks and the olive oil in the well and slowly incorporate the flour until the dough holds together. Knead the dough until smooth, about 5 minutes. Cover the bowl with plastic wrap and let stand at room temperature for 30 minutes.

2. Preheat the oven to 375°F. Brush the flesh of the squash with olive oil and place them, cut-side up, on parchment-lined baking sheets. Place the squash in the oven and roast until fork-tender, 40 to 45 minutes. Remove from the oven and let cool, then scoop the flesh into a bowl and mash until smooth. Add the bread crumbs, cheeses, remaining egg yolks, nutmeg, and rosemary to the squash and stir to thoroughly combine.

3. To begin forming the ravioli, divide the dough into two pieces. Use a pasta maker to roll each piece into a long, thin rectangle. Place one of the rectangles over a floured ravioli tray and spoon a teaspoon of the filling in each of the depressions. Combine the beaten egg and water in a small bowl. Dip a pastry brush or a finger into the wash and lightly coat the edge of each ravioli with it. Gently lay the other rectangle over the piece in the ravioli tray. Use a rolling pin to gently cut out the ravioli. Remove the cut ravioli and place them on a flour-dusted baking sheet.

4. Bring a large saucepan of salted water to a boil. When the water is boiling, add the ravioli, stir to make sure they do not stick to the bottom, and cook until tender but still chewy, about 2 minutes. Drain, divide them between the serving plates, drizzle the Creamy Leek Sauce over the top, and garnish with additional Parmesan.

Spaghetti Squash Noodles with Swiss Chard & Toasted Pecans

YIELD: **4 SERVINGS**

ACTIVE TIME: **30 MINUTES**

TOTAL TIME: **1 HOUR AND 30 MINUTES**

Vegetarian, gluten-free, or omnivore, this dish satisfies all. The meaty, herbal notes of the chard are a nice contrast to the sweet strands of squash.

INGREDIENTS

2 SPAGHETTI SQUASH (ABOUT 2 LBS. EACH)

SALT AND WHITE PEPPER, TO TASTE

1 LB. SWISS CHARD, STEMS REMOVED

½ CUP PECANS

3 TABLESPOONS OLIVE OIL, PLUS 2 TEASPOONS

1 TEASPOON CHILI POWDER

1 TEASPOON SUGAR

2 GARLIC CLOVES, MINCED

½ TEASPOON RED PEPPER FLAKES

1 TABLESPOON FINELY CHOPPED FRESH ROSEMARY

1 TEASPOON CHINESE BLACK VINEGAR

¾ CUP GRATED PARMESAN CHEESE

DIRECTIONS

1. Preheat the oven to 400°F. Line a large baking pan with aluminum foil and trim a sheet of parchment paper so that it fits in the bottom of the pan. Trim the ends of the squash, scrape out the seeds, and cut each of them into four rounds. Place them in the pan, place the pan in the oven, and roast until the strands are tender but still firm, about 50 minutes. Remove from the oven and let cool for 10 minutes.

2. Using a fork, pull the strands in the center of each round to create long strands of "spaghetti." Working in two batches, transfer half of the strands to a kitchen towel and gently wring it to remove as much liquid from the squash as possible. Transfer the squash to a large bowl and repeat this step with the other half of the squash. Set aside.

3. While the squash is roasting, bring a large pot of salted water to a boil. Add the chard leaves and cook until wilted, about 2 minutes. Using a strainer, transfer to a colander and rinse under cold water until cool. Drain well, squeeze the chard to remove as much liquid as possible, and mince. Set aside.

4. Place the pecans in a small resealable bag and gently crush with a rolling pin. Warm a skillet for 3 minutes over low heat. Add the 2 teaspoons of olive oil, the chili powder, and sugar and stir. Once the mixture starts to gently sizzle, add the pecans and stir until coated. Cook until fragrant, about 2 minutes. Season with salt and stir to combine. Transfer to a plate and let cool.

Continued...

5. Warm a large skillet over low heat for 2 to 3 minutes. Add 1 tablespoon of the oil and warm for a minute, then add the garlic, red pepper flakes, rosemary, and a pinch of salt. Cook until the garlic just starts to brown, about 2 minutes. Raise heat to medium-high, add the chard and a pinch of salt, stir to combine, and cook for 3 minutes. Transfer the chard to a warmed bowl and tent with aluminum foil to keep warm. Add the remaining olive oil and let it warm for a minute. Add the spaghetti squash strands and two pinches of salt and toss to coat. Sprinkle the vinegar over the top, season with white pepper, and toss again. Taste and adjust the seasoning as needed. Remove from heat, add the Parmesan, and toss to combine. Divide between four warm bowls and top with the chard and pecans.

INGREDIENTS

2½ LBS. SWEET POTATOES

½ CUP RICOTTA CHEESE

1 EGG

2 EGG YOLKS

1 TABLESPOON KOSHER SALT, PLUS
MORE TO TASTE

1 TEASPOON BLACK PEPPER

3 TABLESPOONS LIGHT BROWN
SUGAR

2 TABLESPOONS REAL MAPLE SYRUP

2 CUPS ALL-PURPOSE FLOUR, PLUS
MORE AS NEEDED

1 CUP SEMOLINA FLOUR

2 TABLESPOONS OLIVE OIL

1 STICK UNSALTED BUTTER

1 TABLESPOON CHOPPED SAGE
LEAVES

2 CUPS ARUGULA

½ CUP TOASTED WALNUTS,
CHOPPED

Sweet Potato Gnocchi with Sage Brown Butter

YIELD: **6 SERVINGS**

ACTIVE TIME: **1 HOUR**

TOTAL TIME: **2 HOURS AND 30 MINUTES**

Sweet potatoes and ricotta make these dumplings both hearty and airy.

DIRECTIONS

1. Preheat the oven to 350°F. Wash the sweet potatoes, place them on a parchment-lined baking sheet, and use a knife to pierce several holes in the tops of the potatoes. Place in the oven and cook until they are soft all the way through, 45 minutes to 1 hour. Remove from the oven, slice them open, and let cool completely.

2. Scrape the cooled sweet potato flesh into a mixing bowl and mash until smooth. Add the ricotta, egg, egg yolks, salt, pepper, brown sugar, and maple syrup and stir until thoroughly combined. Add the flours 1 cup at a time and work the mixture with your hands until incorporated. The dough should not feel sticky when touched. If it is too sticky, add more all-purpose flour 1 teaspoon at a time until it has the right texture. Place the olive oil in a mixing bowl and set aside.

3. Transfer the dough to a lightly floured work surface and cut into 10 even pieces. Roll each piece into a long rope and cut the ropes into ¾-inch pieces. Use a fork to roll the gnocchi into the desired shape and place the shaped dumplings on a lightly floured baking sheet.

4. Bring a large pot of salted water to boil. Working in small batches, add the gnocchi to the boiling water and stir to keep them from sticking to the bottom. The gnocchi will eventually float to the surface. Cook for 1 more minute, remove, and transfer to the bowl containing the olive oil. Toss to coat and place on a parchment-lined baking sheet to cool.

5. Place the butter in a skillet and cook over medium heat until it begins to brown. Add the sage and cook until the bubbles start to dissipate. Place the arugula in a bowl and set aside.

6. Working in batches, add the gnocchi to the skillet, toss to coat, and cook until they have a nice sear on one side. Transfer to the bowl of arugula and toss to combine. Plate and top with the toasted walnuts.

Spring Risotto

YIELD: **4 SERVINGS**

ACTIVE TIME: **45 MINUTES**

TOTAL TIME: **1 HOUR**

The fennel, shallot, and fontina are background notes that offer sweetness and body to this wonderfully fresh risotto.

INGREDIENTS

½ CUP CHOPPED FRESH CHIVES

½ CUP OLIVE OIL, PLUS 2 TABLESPOONS

½ TEASPOON KOSHER SALT, PLUS MORE TO TASTE

½ LB. ASPARAGUS, TRIMMED

2 CUPS VEGETABLE STOCK (SEE PAGE 12)

1 TABLESPOON UNSALTED BUTTER

2 TABLESPOONS CHOPPED SHALLOT

½ CUP MINCED FENNEL

1 CUP ARBORIO RICE

¼ CUP DRY WHITE WINE

¼ CUP GRATED FONTINA CHEESE, PLUS MORE FOR GARNISH

BLACK PEPPER, TO TASTE

1 TABLESPOON FRESH LEMON JUICE

4 OZ. MUSHROOMS, TRIMMED

DIRECTIONS

1. Preheat the oven to 400°F. Place the chives, the ½ cup of olive oil, and salt in a blender and puree in smooth. Set aside.

2. Place the asparagus on a baking sheet, place it in the oven, and roast until tender, 15 to 20 minutes. Remove the asparagus from the oven and briefly let cool. Chop the asparagus into 1-inch pieces and set aside.

3. Place the stock in a small saucepan and bring to a simmer over medium heat. Turn off the heat and leave the pan on the stove. Place the butter and 1 tablespoon of the remaining olive oil in a large skillet and warm over medium heat. Add the shallot and fennel and sauté until they just start to brown, about 5 minutes. Add the rice and toast it until it starts to give off a nutty aroma, while stirring constantly.

4. Deglaze the pan with the white wine and scrape up any browned bits from the bottom. When the wine has been fully absorbed by the rice, add the warm stock a little at a time, stirring constantly to prevent sticking, and cook until the rice absorbs it. If the rice is still crunchy by the time you have used up all of the stock, incorporate water in 1-tablespoon increments until it reaches the desired tenderness.

5. When the rice is a few minutes from being done—still a little too firm—stir in the asparagus. When the rice is al dente, stir in the cheese, season with salt and pepper, and add the lemon juice. Stir to incorporate and turn off the heat.

Continued...

6. Place remaining oil in a large skillet, warm over medium-high heat, and then add the mushrooms in one layer. Add a pinch of salt and cook until the mushrooms start to brown, about 5 minutes. Turn the mushrooms over, add another pinch of salt, and cook for another 5 minutes. Divide the risotto between four warmed bowls and top each portion with a few mushrooms. Drizzle the chive-infused oil over the top and sprinkle additional fontina on top.

Tofu Tacos

The seasoning amounts should be used as a guide rather than a hard rule, depending on your spice threshold.

INGREDIENTS

1 TABLESPOON OLIVE OIL, PLUS MORE AS NEEDED

1 LB. EXTRA-FIRM TOFU, DRAINED AND CRUMBLED

1 TABLESPOON KOSHER SALT

1 TABLESPOON CUMIN

1 TABLESPOON GARLIC POWDER

1 TABLESPOON CAYENNE POWDER

ADOBO SAUCE, TO TASTE

CORN TORTILLAS (SEE PAGE 40), FOR SERVING

PREFERRED TOPPINGS, FOR SERVING

DIRECTIONS

1. Place the oil in a large skillet and warm over medium-high heat. Once the oil is shimmering, add the tofu and all of the seasonings. Stir until the tofu is thoroughly coated and then cook until it starts to brown, about 5 minutes.

2. Scramble the tofu in the pan and cook until it is browned all over, about 5 minutes.

3. Add the adobo sauce and more oil if the pan looks dry. Cook for 5 more minutes and then serve with the Corn Tortillas and the toppings of your choice.

Polenta with Corn, Peppers & Tomatillos

YIELD: **4 SERVINGS**

ACTIVE TIME: **25 MINUTES**

TOTAL TIME: **40 MINUTES**

This meal hits all the right notes. The creamy polenta is the perfect complement to the sweet-and-sour elements added by the tomatillos. Add the jalapeño if you like things spicy.

INGREDIENTS

1 TABLESPOON OLIVE OIL, PLUS MORE AS NEEDED

1 ONION, DICED

1 CUP CORN KERNELS

½ SWEET PEPPER, STEMMED, SEEDED, AND CHOPPED

1 SMALL JALAPEÑO PEPPER, STEMMED, SEEDED, AND CHOPPED (OPTIONAL)

½ LB. TOMATILLOS, HUSKED, RINSED, AND CHOPPED

1 TEASPOON CUMIN

1½ TEASPOONS KOSHER SALT

1 GARLIC CLOVE, MINCED

1 CUP MILK

2 CUPS WATER, PLUS MORE AS NEEDED

1 CUP MEDIUM-GRAIN CORNMEAL

2 TABLESPOONS UNSALTED BUTTER

1 CUP GRATED CHEDDAR CHEESE, PLUS MORE FOR GARNISH

¼ CUP FINELY CHOPPED FRESH CILANTRO, FOR GARNISH

DIRECTIONS

1. Place the oil in a large skillet and warm over medium-high heat. When the oil starts to shimmer, add the onion and sauté until it starts to brown, about 10 minutes. Add the corn and continue to cook, adding more oil if the pan becomes too dry. When the corn has started to brown, add the pepper, jalapeno (if using), tomatillos, cumin, and 1 teaspoon of the salt. Cook until the tomatillos start to collapse, about 5 minutes. Add the garlic and cook until fragrant, about 2 minutes. Remove the pan from heat and set aside.

2. Place the milk, water, and remaining salt in a medium saucepan and bring it to a boil. Add the cornmeal slowly, while stirring constantly to prevent lumps from forming. Reduce the heat to a simmer and cooking, stirring continuously. Continue until all of the liquid is absorbed and the cornmeal is tender, about 10 minutes. If the polenta absorbs all of the water before it is cooked, add up to 1 cup water.

3. Add the butter and cheese to the polenta and stir to combine. To serve, ladle the polenta onto a plate and top with a large spoonful of the corn-and-tomatillo mixture. Garnish with the cilantro and additional cheddar cheese.

Green Shakshuka

YIELD: **4 SERVINGS**

ACTIVE TIME: **20 MINUTES**

TOTAL TIME: **30 MINUTES**

Here, tomatillos add a tangy note to the mild spinach and eggs. The Tabasco is optional, but highly recommended to finish this dish off.

INGREDIENTS

1 TABLESPOON OLIVE OIL

1 ONION, CHOPPED

2 GARLIC CLOVES, MINCED

½ LB. TOMATILLOS, HUSKED, RINSED, AND CHOPPED

1 (12 OZ.) PACKAGE FROZEN CHOPPED SPINACH

1 TEASPOON CORIANDER

¼ CUP WATER

SALT AND PEPPER, TO TASTE

4 EGGS

TABASCO, FOR SERVING (OPTIONAL)

DIRECTIONS

1. Place the oil in a large skillet and warm over medium-high heat. When the oil starts to shimmer, add the onion and sauté until just starting to soften, about 5 minutes. Add the garlic and cook until fragrant, about 2 minutes. Add the tomatillos and cook until they have collapsed, about 5 minutes.

2. Add the spinach, coriander, and water and cook, breaking up the spinach with a fork, until the spinach is completely defrosted and blended with the tomatillos. Season with salt and pepper.

3. Evenly spread the mixture in the pan and then make four indentations in it. Crack an egg into each indentation. Reduce the heat to medium, cover the pan, and let the eggs cook until the whites set, 3 to 5 minutes. Serve with Tabasco, if desired.

Eggplant Parmesan

This recipe bakes the eggplant instead of frying it, which cuts down on the grease significantly.

YIELD: **4 SERVINGS**

ACTIVE TIME: **20 MINUTES**

TOTAL TIME: **1 HOUR AND 45 MINUTES**

INGREDIENTS

1 LARGE EGGPLANT

SALT, TO TASTE

2 TABLESPOONS OLIVE OIL

1 CUP ITALIAN-SEASONED BREAD CRUMBS

2 TABLESPOONS GRATED PARMESAN CHEESE

1 EGG, BEATEN

MARINARA SAUCE (SEE PAGE 27), AS NEEDED

2 GARLIC CLOVES, MINCED

½ LB. MOZZARELLA CHEESE, GRATED

FRESH BASIL, FINELY CHOPPED, FOR GARNISH

DIRECTIONS

1. Preheat the oven to 350°F. Trim the top and bottom off the eggplant and slice into ¼-inch-thick slices. Put the slices on paper towels in a single layer, sprinkle salt over them, and let rest for about 15 minutes. Turn the slices over, salt the other side, and let sit for another 15 minutes. Rinse the salt from all the pieces and pat them dry with paper towels.

2. Drizzle the oil over a baking sheet. In a shallow bowl, combine the bread crumbs and Parmesan cheese. Put the beaten egg in another shallow bowl. Dip the slices of eggplant in the egg and then in the bread crumb-and-cheese mixture until both sides are coated. Place the breaded slices on the baking sheet.

3. When all of the eggplant has been breaded, place it in the oven and bake for 10 minutes. Remove, turn the slices over, and bake for another 10 minutes. Remove the sheet from the oven and let cool slightly.

4. Place a layer of sauce in a baking dish or a cast-iron skillet and stir in the garlic. Lay some of the eggplant slices on top of the sauce, top them with more sauce, and then place the remaining eggplant on top. Top with the grated mozzarella.

5. Place in the oven and bake for about 30 minutes, until the sauce is bubbling and the cheese is golden brown. Remove from the oven and let cool for 10 minutes before serving with additional Marinara Sauce and fresh basil.

CHAPTER 7

DESSERTS

Having taken your cooking to another level, you've earned the right to treat yourself. Considering all you've learned, however, there's no reason to take things outside the home and head to the store or bakery when it comes to provide something special for the all-important last course.

Whether it be a simple, delicious preparations such as a classic Carrot Cake (see page 303), or the Strawberry Rhubarb Ricotta Cakes with Lemon Meringue (see page 315) that will turn everyone's head as you bring them to the table, many of these desserts require you to go no further than your garden and pantry to procure the ingredients. And by relying on the natural sweetness and tartness that Mother Nature remains an unparalleled producer of, you once again will open people's eyes to the wonders that can be wrested from the ground.

Perfect Piecrusts

This piecrust recipe is guaranteed to provide the light, flaky result you want.

YIELD: **2 PIECRUSTS**

ACTIVE TIME: **15 MINUTES**

TOTAL TIME: **2 HOURS AND 15 MINUTES**

INGREDIENTS

2½ CUPS ALL-PURPOSE FLOUR

1½ TABLESPOONS SUGAR

1 TEASPOON KOSHER SALT

¾ CUP VEGETABLE SHORTENING

2 TABLESPOONS UNSALTED BUTTER, CHILLED AND DIVIDED INTO TABLESPOONS

5 TABLESPOONS ICE-COLD WATER, PLUS MORE AS NEEDED

DIRECTIONS

1. Place the flour, sugar, and salt in a bowl and stir until combined.

2. Add the shortening and butter and use a pastry blender to work them into the flour mixture. Work the mixture until it is a coarse meal, making sure to break up any large chunks.

3. Add the water and continue to work the mixture until it is a smooth dough. If it feels too dry, incorporate water in 1-teaspoon increments. Form the dough into a large ball and then cut it in half. Wrap each piece in plastic wrap and place in the refrigerator for 2 hours before using. The dough will keep in the refrigerator for up to 3 days. It also freezes very well, and can be stored in a freezer for up to 6 months.

Tart Pastry Shell

Prebaking the shells for your tarts saves you time and guarantees that they never become soggy when filled.

YIELD: **9-INCH PASTRY SHELL**

ACTIVE TIME: **30 MINUTES**

TOTAL TIME: **3 HOURS AND 15 MINUTES**

INGREDIENTS

1 LARGE EGG YOLK

1 TABLESPOON HEAVY CREAM

½ TEASPOON PURE VANILLA EXTRACT

1¼ CUPS ALL-PURPOSE FLOUR, PLUS MORE FOR DUSTING

⅔ CUP CONFECTIONERS' SUGAR

¼ TEASPOON KOSHER SALT

1 STICK UNSALTED BUTTER, CUT INTO 4 PIECES

DIRECTIONS

1. Place the egg yolk, cream, and vanilla in a small bowl, whisk to combine, and set aside. Place the flour, sugar, and salt in a food processor and pulse to combine. Add the pieces of butter and pulse until the mixture resembles a coarse meal. Set the food processor to puree and add the egg mixture as it is running. Puree until the dough just comes together, about 20 seconds. Place the dough on a sheet of plastic wrap, press it into 6-inch disk, wrap, and refrigerate for at least 2 hours.

2. Approximately 1 hour before you are planning to start constructing your tart, remove the dough from the refrigerator. Lightly dust a large sheet of parchment paper or plastic wrap with flour and place the dough in the center. Roll out to 9 inches and line a greased tart pan with it. Place the pan containing the rolled-out dough in the freezer.

3. Preheat the oven to 375°F. Place the chilled tart shell on a baking sheet, line the inside of the tart shell with aluminum foil, and fill with uncooked rice. Bake for 30 minutes, rotating the shell halfway through.

4. After 30 minutes, remove the shell from the oven and discard the rice and foil. Leave the tart shell on the baking sheet and place it on the upper rack of the oven. Bake until the shell is golden brown, about 5 minutes. Remove and fill as desired.

Caramelized Peach Custard Tart

YIELD: **6 TO 8 SERVINGS**

ACTIVE TIME: **25 MINUTES**

TOTAL TIME: **1 HOUR**

Pairing the exceptional sweetness of caramelized peaches with an elegant custard makes for a memorable dessert.

INGREDIENTS

2 TABLESPOONS UNSALTED BUTTER

2 LARGE PEACHES, PITTED AND SLICED

7 TABLESPOONS SUGAR

¼ TEASPOON CINNAMON

2 TABLESPOONS BRANDY

½ CUP MILK

½ CUP HEAVY CREAM

2 EGGS

1 EGG YOLK

½ TEASPOON PURE VANILLA EXTRACT

¼ TEASPOON KOSHER SALT

1 TART PASTRY SHELL (SEE PAGE 295)

DIRECTIONS

1. Place the butter in a skillet and melt over medium-high heat. Add the peaches to the melted butter and cook, turning the slices as they cook, until they are brown on all sides.

2. Sprinkle 3 tablespoons of the sugar over the peaches and shake the pan until they are evenly coated. Cook until the peaches start to caramelize, about 10 minutes.

3. Tilt the pan away from you, add the brandy, and use a long match or a long-handled lighter to ignite the brandy. Shake the pan until the alcohol cooks off and then pour the mixture into a heatproof mixing bowl. Let the mixture cool.

4. Preheat the oven to 300°F. When the flambéed peaches are close to cool, place the milk, heavy cream, eggs, egg yolk, remaining sugar, vanilla, and salt in a mixing bowl and whisk to combine.

5. Evenly distribute the flambéed peaches in the pastry shell and then strain the custard over the top. Place the tart in the oven and bake until the custard is just set, 20 to 25 minutes. Remove from the oven and let cool before serving.

INGREDIENTS

FOR THE COCONUT BUTTERCREAM FROSTING

4 LARGE EGG WHITES

1 CUP SUGAR

1 PINCH KOSHER SALT

4 STICKS UNSALTED BUTTER, CUT INTO SMALL PIECES AND AT ROOM TEMPERATURE

¼ CUP CREAM OF COCONUT

1 TEASPOON PURE VANILLA EXTRACT

FOR THE CAKE

2¼ CUPS CAKE FLOUR, SIFTED, PLUS MORE FOR DUSTING

1 CUP SUGAR

1 TABLESPOON BAKING POWDER

¾ TEASPOON KOSHER SALT

1½ STICKS UNSALTED BUTTER, DIVIDED INTO TABLESPOONS AND AT ROOM TEMPERATURE

5 LARGE EGG WHITES

1 LARGE EGG

1 TEASPOON PURE VANILLA EXTRACT

¾ CUP CREAM OF COCONUT

¼ CUP WATER

2 CUPS SWEETENED SHREDDED COCONUT

Coconut Layer Cake

YIELD: **8 TO 10 SERVINGS**

ACTIVE TIME: **35 MINUTES**

TOTAL TIME: **1 HOUR AND 30 MINUTES**

Placing light and sweet coconut buttercream between the layers of cake makes this a dreamy delight.

DIRECTIONS

1. Preheat the oven to 350°F and grease two round 9-inch cake pans with nonstick cooking spray.

2. To prepare the frosting, place 2 inches of water in a saucepan and bring to a gentle simmer. Place the egg whites, sugar, and salt in a metal mixing bowl and place the bowl over the saucepan. Cook, while whisking constantly, for about 2 minutes. Remove the bowl from heat and beat the mixture until it is shiny. Incorporate the butter one piece at a time. Add the cream of coconut and vanilla extract and beat until well combined. Scrape down the bowl as needed while mixing. Set aside.

3. To begin preparations for the cake, place the flour, sugar, baking powder, and salt in a mixing bowl and whisk to combine. Incorporate the butter one piece at a time and work the mixture with a pastry blender until the mixture resembles a coarse meal.

4. Place the egg whites and the egg in a separate bowl and beat until combined. Add the vanilla, cream of coconut, and water and beat until well combined.

5. Add half of the wet mixture to the dry mixture and beat until light and fluffy. Slowly add the remaining half of the wet mixture and beat until incorporated. Scrape down the bowl as needed.

6. Divide the batter between the prepared pans, place in the oven, and bake until they are golden brown and a toothpick inserted into the center of each comes out clean, about 25 minutes. Remove from the oven and let the cakes cool in the pan for 10 minutes.

7. Place the cakes on wire racks and let cool to room temperature.

8. When the cakes are cool, spread some of the frosting over the top of one of the cakes. Place the other cake on top, bottom-side up, and spread the remaining frosting over the entire cake. Sprinkle the shredded coconut over the top and serve.

Date & Toffee Pudding Cakes

YIELD: **8 SERVINGS**

ACTIVE TIME: **45 MINUTES**

TOTAL TIME: **1 HOUR AND 30 MINUTES**

It may take a few tries to get the texture just right, but once you do, these rich cakes will become one of your favorite dishes.

INGREDIENTS

¾ CUP WARM WATER (110°F), PLUS 1 TABLESPOON

½ TEASPOON BAKING SODA

½ LB. PITTED DATES, CHOPPED

1¼ CUPS ALL-PURPOSE FLOUR

½ TEASPOON BAKING POWDER

¾ TEASPOON KOSHER SALT

1¾ CUPS FIRMLY PACKED DARK BROWN SUGAR

2 LARGE EGGS

1 STICK UNSALTED BUTTER, HALF MELTED, HALF AT ROOM TEMPERATURE

1½ TABLESPOONS PURE VANILLA EXTRACT

1 CUP HEAVY CREAM

1 DASH FRESH LEMON JUICE

DIRECTIONS

1. Place the ¾ cup of warm water, baking soda, and half of the dates in a large mason jar and soak for 5 minutes. Make sure the liquid is covering the dates.

2. Preheat the oven to 350°F and grease eight 4 oz. ramekins with nonstick cooking spray. Bring water to boil in a small saucepan.

3. Place the flour, baking powder, and ½ teaspoon of the salt in a mixing bowl and whisk to combine.

4. Place ¾ cup of the brown sugar and the remaining dates in a blender or food processor and blitz until the mixture is fine. Drain the soaked dates, reserve the liquid, and set them aside. Add the reserved liquid to the blender along with the eggs, melted butter, and vanilla and puree until smooth. Add the puree and soaked dates to the flour mixture and fold to combine.

5. Fill each ramekin two-thirds of the way with the batter, place the filled ramekins in a large roasting pan, and pour the boiling water in the roasting pan so that it goes halfway up each ramekin.

6. Cover tightly with aluminum foil and place the pan in the oven. Bake until each cake is puffy and the surfaces are spongy but firm, about 40 minutes. Remove the ramekins from the roasting pan and let cool on a wire rack for 10 minutes.

Continued...

7. Place the remaining butter in a saucepan and warm over medium-high heat. When the butter
    is melted, add the remaining brown sugar and salt and whisk until smooth. Cook, while stirring
    occasionally, until the brown sugar has dissolved. Slowly add the cream, while stirring constantly,
    until it has all been incorporated and the mixture is smooth. Reduce heat to low and simmer until the
    mixture starts to bubble. Remove from heat and stir in the lemon juice.

8. To serve, invert each cake into a bowl or onto a dish, spoon a generous amount of the sauce over
    each, and serve.

CREAM CHEESE FROSTING

Place an 8-ounce package of cream cheese, 5 tablespoons unsalted butter, 1 tablespoon sour cream, and ½ teaspoon of pure vanilla extract in a food processor and blitz until combined. Scrape down the bowl as needed. Add 1¼ cups confectioners' sugar, blitz until the frosting is smooth, and refrigerate until ready to use.

Carrot Cake

YIELD: **6 TO 8 SERVINGS**

ACTIVE TIME: **20 MINUTES**

TOTAL TIME: **2 HOURS AND 15 MINUTES**

This classic dessert can also help you cut down on food waste—just store your carrot trimmings in the freezer and pull them out when it's time to make this.

INGREDIENTS

2 CUPS SHREDDED CARROTS, PLUS MORE FOR TOPPING

2 CUPS SUGAR

1½ CUPS ALL-PURPOSE FLOUR

1½ TABLESPOONS BAKING SODA

1 TEASPOON KOSHER SALT

1 TABLESPOON CINNAMON

3 EGGS

1¾ CUPS VEGETABLE OIL

2 TEASPOONS PURE VANILLA EXTRACT

½ CUP WALNUTS, CHOPPED (OPTIONAL)

CREAM CHEESE FROSTING (SEE SIDEBAR)

DIRECTIONS

1. Preheat the oven to 350°F. Place the carrots and sugar in a mixing bowl, stir to combine, and let the mixture sit for 10 minutes.

2. Place the flour, baking soda, salt, and cinnamon in a mixing bowl and stir to combine. Place the eggs, vegetable oil, and vanilla extract in a separate mixing bowl and stir to combine. Add the wet mixture to the dry mixture and stir until the mixture is a smooth batter. Stir in the carrots and, if desired, the walnuts.

3. Transfer the batter to a greased 9-inch cake pan and place the cake in the oven. Bake until the top is browned and a knife inserted into the center comes out clean, about 40 to 50 minutes.

4. Remove the cake from the oven, transfer to a wire rack, and let cool for 1 hour before applying the frosting. Top each slice with additional shredded carrot before serving.

Rosé Sorbet

Unwinding with a glass of chilled Rosé on a hot day is one of the ultimate summer pastimes. Combine it with another beloved summer staple—frozen treats—and you can't go wrong.

YIELD: **6 SERVINGS**

ACTIVE TIME: **10 MINUTES**

TOTAL TIME: **24 HOURS**

INGREDIENTS

1⅓ CUPS SUGAR

1 (750 ML) BOTTLE OF ROSÉ

1 CUP WATER

DIRECTIONS

1. Place all of the ingredients in a saucepan and cook, while stirring, over medium-low heat until the sugar has dissolved. Raise the heat and bring to a boil.

2. Remove from heat and let cool completely. Cover and place the mixture in the refrigerator overnight.

3. Pour the mixture into an ice cream maker and churn until the desired texture has been reached.

4. Transfer to the freezer and freeze for at least 4 hours before serving, though 8 to 10 hours in the freezer is recommended.

   NOTE: An ice cream maker is a must for this and the other ice cream-adjacent preparations in this book. While not an essential kitchen appliance, a more-than-serviceable one from Cuisinart is available for around $40.

Roasted Parsnip Ice Cream

YIELD: **6 SERVINGS**

ACTIVE TIME: **20 MINUTES**

TOTAL TIME: **24 HOURS**

The unique and surprising sweetness of parsnips finally gets a stage fit for its talents with this ice cream.

INGREDIENTS

1½ CUPS HEAVY CREAM

1½ CUPS WHOLE MILK

3 TO 4 CUPS OF ROASTED PARSNIP TRIMMINGS (THE STUFF YOU TYPICALLY THROW AWAY)

1 PINCH KOSHER SALT

⅔ CUP SUGAR

5 EGG YOLKS

DIRECTIONS

1. Place the cream, milk, roasted parsnip pieces, and salt in a saucepan and cook over medium heat until the mixture starts to bubble. Remove it from heat and allow the mixture to steep for 30 minutes to 1 hour.

2. Strain the mixture through a fine sieve, while pressing down on the pieces of parsnip to remove as much liquid as possible. Place the liquid in a saucepan and bring to a simmer. Discard the parsnip pieces.

3. Place the sugar and egg yolks in a bowl and whisk until combined.

4. Once the liquid is simmering, add a little bit of it to the egg-and-sugar mixture and whisk constantly. Add the liquid in small increments until all of it has been incorporated, while taking care not to cook the eggs.

5. Return the tempered eggs to the saucepan and cook over low heat, while stirring, until it is thick enough to coat the back of a wooden spoon. Remove from heat and let cool. When cool, cover and transfer to the refrigerator. Chill overnight.

6. When you are ready to make ice cream, add the mixture to your ice cream maker and churn until the desired consistency has been achieved. Place the churned cream in the freezer for at least 6 hours before serving.

Black Raspberry Ice Cream

Make sure you get black raspberries and not blackberries, as the former is less tart and fruitier.

YIELD: **4 CUPS**

ACTIVE TIME: **30 MINUTES**

TOTAL TIME: **24 HOURS**

INGREDIENTS

2½ CUPS HEAVY CREAM

1½ CUPS WHOLE MILK

1 CUP SUGAR

SALT, TO TASTE

6 LARGE EGG YOLKS

1 TEASPOON PURE VANILLA EXTRACT

5 CUPS BLACK RASPBERRIES

DIRECTIONS

1. Place the cream, milk, sugar, and salt in a saucepan, warm over medium heat until it starts to bubble, and remove from heat. Take care not to let the mixture come to a boil.

2. Place the egg yolks in a heatproof mixing bowl and whisk to combine. While whisking constantly, add one-third of the warm milk mixture to the egg yolks. When incorporated, whisk the tempered egg yolks into the saucepan.

3. Cook over medium-low heat, while stirring constantly, until the mixture is thick enough to coat the back of a wooden spoon, about 5 minutes. Take care not to let the mixture come to a boil. Strain through a fine mesh sieve and stir in the vanilla. Set the mixture aside.

4. Place the raspberries in a blender and puree until smooth. Strain through a fine sieve to remove the seeds and then stir the puree into the custard. Cover and place in the refrigerator to chill overnight.

5. Pour the mixture in an ice cream maker and churn until the desired consistency is achieved. Place in the freezer for 6 hours before serving.

Chocolate Cheesecake Tart

YIELD: **6 TO 8 SERVINGS**

ACTIVE TIME: **40 MINUTES**

TOTAL TIME: **7 HOURS AND 30 MINUTES**

A whole lot of flavor for not too much effort.

INGREDIENTS

8 TO 10 OREO COOKIES, FILLING SCRAPED OFF

2 TABLESPOONS UNSWEETENED COCOA POWDER

2 TABLESPOONS KAHLÙA

1 STICK UNSALTED BUTTER, MELTED

2 (8 OZ.) PACKAGES OF CREAM CHEESE, AT ROOM TEMPERATURE

1 CUP SUGAR

½ TEASPOON PURE VANILLA EXTRACT

2 EGGS

DIRECTIONS

1. Preheat the oven to 350°F. Place the cookies in a food processor or blender and pulse until they are crumbs. You can also put the cookies in a large resealable plastic bag and use a rolling pin to crush them.

2. Place the crumbs in a large bowl and add 1 tablespoon of the unsweetened cocoa powder, the Kahlùa, and butter. Stir until combined and then press the mixture into a greased 9-inch springform pan. Place the pan in the oven and bake until the crust is firm, about 10 minutes. Remove the pan from the oven and let it cool. Reduce oven temperature to 325°F.

3. Place the cream cheese and sugar in the mixing bowl of a stand mixer fitted with the paddle attachment. Beat on medium speed until low. Add the remaining cocoa powder, the vanilla, and eggs and beat until they have been incorporated.

4. Scrape the mixture into the cooled crust, put the tart in the oven, and bake until the filling is set, about 40 minutes. Remove from the oven, briefly allow to cool, and refrigerate for 6 hours before serving.

Dutch Apple Baby

A quick dessert that looks irresistible when brought to the table in a cast-iron skillet.

YIELD: **4 SERVINGS**

ACTIVE TIME: **15 MINUTES**

TOTAL TIME: **40 MINUTES**

INGREDIENTS

4 TABLESPOONS UNSALTED BUTTER

2 TART APPLES, CORED, PEELED, AND SLICED

¼ CUP SUGAR, PLUS 3 TABLESPOONS

1 TABLESPOON CINNAMON

¾ CUP ALL-PURPOSE FLOUR

¼ TEASPOON KOSHER SALT

¾ CUP MILK

4 EGGS

1 TEASPOON PURE VANILLA EXTRACT

CONFECTIONERS' SUGAR, FOR DUSTING

DIRECTIONS

1. Preheat the oven to 425°F and place a rack in the middle position. Warm a cast-iron skillet over medium-high heat. Add the butter and apples and cook, while stirring, until the apples soften, about 3 to 4 minutes. Add the ¼ cup of sugar and the cinnamon and cook for another 3 to 4 minutes. Distribute the apples evenly over the bottom of the skillet and remove from heat.

2. In a large bowl, mix the remaining sugar, flour, and salt together. In a smaller bowl, whisk together the milk, eggs, and vanilla extract. Add the wet mixture to the dry mixture and stir to combine. Pour the resulting batter over the apples.

3. Place the skillet in the oven and bake until the pastry is puffy and golden brown, about 20 minutes. Remove the skillet from the oven and let cool for a few minutes. Run a knife along the edge of the skillet to loosen the pastry and then, using oven mitts or pot holders, invert it onto a large plate. Dust with the confectioners' sugar and serve warm.

RHUBARB JAM

Place 4 cups chopped rhubarb, 1 cup water, ¾ cup sugar, and ½ teaspoon kosher salt in a saucepan and cook over high heat, stirring occasionally to prevent sticking, until nearly all of the liquid has evaporated. Add 1 teaspoon pectin and stir the mixture for 1 minute. Transfer to a sterilized mason jar and allow to cool completely before applying the lid and placing it in the refrigerator, where the jam will keep for up to 1 week.

INGREDIENTS

FOR THE CAKES

1 STICK UNSALTED BUTTER, AT ROOM TEMPERATURE

½ CUP SUGAR

2 EGGS

¼ TEASPOON PURE VANILLA EXTRACT

ZEST OF 1 LEMON

¾ CUP RICOTTA CHEESE

¾ CUP ALL-PURPOSE FLOUR

1 TEASPOON BAKING POWDER

½ TEASPOON KOSHER SALT

½ CUP MINCED STRAWBERRIES, PLUS MORE FOR GARNISH

½ CUP RHUBARB JAM (SEE SIDEBAR)

FOR THE LEMON MERINGUE

1 CUP SUGAR

½ CUP WATER

4 EGG WHITES

1 TABLESPOON FRESH LEMON JUICE

Strawberry Rhubarb Ricotta Cakes with Lemon Meringue

YIELD: **4 SERVINGS**

ACTIVE TIME: **30 MINUTES**

TOTAL TIME: **1 HOUR AND 15 MINUTES**

The vaunted combination of strawberry and rhubarb isn't only for pies.

DIRECTIONS

1. Preheat the oven to 350°F and grease a 9 x 5-inch loaf pan. To prepare the cakes, place the butter and sugar in the mixing bowl of a stand mixer fitted with the paddle attachment and beat on high until the mixture is smooth and a pale yellow. Reduce speed to medium, add the eggs one at a time, and beat until incorporated. Add the vanilla, lemon zest, and ricotta and beat until the mixture is smooth.

2. Place the flour, baking powder, and salt in a mixing bowl and whisk to combine. Reduce the speed of the mixer to low, add the dry mixture to the wet mixture, and beat until incorporated. Scrape the mixing bowl as needed while mixing the batter.

3. Add the strawberries and fold to incorporate. Place the batter in the loaf pan, place it in the oven, and bake until a toothpick inserted into the center comes out clean, about 35 minutes. Remove from the oven and let cool to room temperature in the pan.

4. To prepare the meringue, place the sugar and water in a saucepan and cook on high until the mixture is 240°F. While the simple syrup is heating up, place the egg whites and lemon juice in the mixing bowl of the stand mixer fitted with the whisk attachment. Beat at medium speed until soft peaks form, about 2 to 3 minutes.

5. When the simple syrup reaches 240°F, slowly add it to the beaten egg whites with the mixer running. Raise the speed to high and beat until stiff peaks form. To test whether the meringue is ready, remove the whisk attachment and turn it so that the whisk is facing up. The meringue should hold its shape. If desired, transfer the meringue to a pastry bag fitted with a piping tip.

6. Remove the cooled cake from the pan and cut it into 8 equal pieces. Spread some of the Rhubarb Jam over four of the pieces. Cover the jam with some of the meringue and then place the unadorned pieces of cake on top. Spread more meringue on top and toast with a pastry torch until golden brown. Garnish with additional strawberries and serve.

Tang Yuan Dango

YIELD: **4 TO 6 SERVINGS**

ACTIVE TIME: **30 MINUTES**

TOTAL TIME: **2 HOURS**

Topping these sweet rice dumplings with freeze-dried berries adds a burst of color and flavor.

INGREDIENTS

4 CUPS FRESH STRAWBERRIES, HULLED AND CHOPPED

1¼ CUPS SUGAR

1½ CUPS SWEET RICE FLOUR (GLUTINOUS RICE FLOUR), PLUS MORE AS NEEDED

⅓ CUP WATER, PLUS MORE AS NEEDED

2 TABLESPOONS CANOLA OIL

6 WOODEN SKEWERS

FREEZE-DRIED STRAWBERRIES, FOR GARNISH

DIRECTIONS

1. Place the strawberries and sugar in a glass mixing bowl and stir to combine. Place 1 inch of water in a small saucepan and bring it to a boil. Cover the bowl with aluminum foil, place it over the saucepan, and let cook for 1 hour. Check the water level every 15 minutes and add more if it has evaporated. After 1 hour, turn off the heat and let the syrup cool. When cool, strain and discard the solids.

2. Bring water to a boil in a large pot. Place the flour, water, and ¾ cup of the syrup in a large mixing bowl and use a fork to work the mixture until combined and very dry. Remove 2 separate tablespoons of the mixture and roll each tablespoon into a ball. Place the balls in the boiling water and cook until they float to the surface and double in size, about 5 minutes. Return the balls to the mixture, add the canola oil, and use the fork to incorporate.

3. Bring the water back to a boil and prepare an ice water bath. Place the mixture on a work surface and knead until it is a smooth and slightly tacky dough. If the dough is too dry or too sticky, incorporate water or flour as needed.

4. Divide the dough into 18 pieces, roll them into balls, and use a slotted spoon to gently lower them into the pot. Gently stir to keep them from sticking to the bottom and then cook until they float to the surface and double in size, about 8 minutes. Remove with a slotted spoon, refresh in the ice water bath, drain, and place 3 balls on each of the skewers. Garnish with the freeze-dried strawberries and drizzle some of the remaining syrup over the top.

Chai-Poached Pears

The always overlooked pear gets its day in the sun with this inventive dessert.

YIELD: **4 SERVINGS**

ACTIVE TIME: **20 MINUTES**

TOTAL TIME: **1 HOUR AND 30 MINUTES**

INGREDIENTS

3 BAGS CHAI TEA

2 CINNAMON STICKS

4 WHOLE CLOVES

2 TEASPOONS GRATED FRESH NUTMEG

½ CUP SUGAR

4 RIPE PEARS, LEFT WHOLE OR PEELED AND SLICED

DIRECTIONS

1. Bring a saucepan of water to a boil. Add the tea bags, cinnamon sticks, cloves, and nutmeg, reduce the heat, and simmer for 10 minutes. Turn off the heat and let mixture steep for 30 minutes.

2. Remove the spices and tea bags from the water. Add the sugar and cook over low heat, while stirring, until the sugar is dissolved. Place the pears in the simmering tea and cook, while spooning the tea over them, until they are tender, about 40 minutes. Turn the pears in the water as they cook to ensure that they are cooked evenly.

3. Remove the pears from liquid, transfer them to the serving dishes, spoon some of the liquid over the top, and serve.

Pumpkin Pie

YIELD: **6 TO 8 SERVINGS**

ACTIVE TIME: **15 MINUTES**

TOTAL TIME: **1 HOUR AND 30 MINUTES**

No need to wait until the holidays to enjoy this smooth, flavorful favorite. It's good anytime, but it may just be best in the morning, with a cup of coffee, in a quiet house.

INGREDIENTS

1 (14 OZ.) CAN PUMPKIN PUREE (NOT PUMPKIN PIE FILLING)

1 (12 OZ.) CAN EVAPORATED MILK

2 EGGS, LIGHTLY BEATEN

½ CUP GRANULATED SUGAR

½ TEASPOON KOSHER SALT

1 TEASPOON CINNAMON

¼ TEASPOON GROUND GINGER

¼ TEASPOON GROUND NUTMEG

1 PERFECT PIECRUST (SEE PAGE 292), BLIND BAKED (SEE SIDEBAR)

DIRECTIONS

1. Preheat the oven to 400°F. In a large bowl, combine the pumpkin puree, evaporated milk, eggs, sugar, salt, cinnamon, ginger, and nutmeg. Stir until thoroughly combined.

2. Working with the crust in the pie plate, fill it with the pumpkin mixture. Smooth the surface with a rubber spatula.

3. Put the pie in the oven and bake for 15 minutes. Reduce the heat to 325°F and bake for an additional 30 to 45 minutes, until the filling is firm and a toothpick inserted in the middle comes out clean. Remove the pie from the oven and let cool before serving.

BLIND BAKING

The technique of baking a piecrust before filling it is also known as "blind baking." When working with a custard filling, as in a lemon meringue or pumpkin pie, baking the crust ahead of time has several advantages. It prevents pockets of steam from forming in the crust once it is filled, which can cause the crust to become puffy and uneven. Blind baking also keeps the bottom of the crust from becoming soggy, and allows the edge of the pie to be sturdy. Uncooked rice is the most typical weight when blind baking a pie, though dried beans and weights designed specifically for the task can also be utilized.

Sweet Potato Pie

One of many dishes devotees of Southern cuisine have had to themselves for years. Lucky for you, the secret's finally out.

YIELD: **6 TO 8 SERVINGS**

ACTIVE TIME: **25 MINUTES**

TOTAL TIME: **2 HOURS**

INGREDIENTS

2 CUPS COOKED AND MASHED SWEET POTATOES

1½ CUPS EVAPORATED MILK

2 EGGS, LIGHTLY BEATEN

½ CUP GRANULATED SUGAR

½ TEASPOON KOSHER SALT

1 TEASPOON CINNAMON

¼ TEASPOON GROUND GINGER

¼ TEASPOON GROUND NUTMEG

1 STICK UNSALTED BUTTER

1 CUP LIGHT BROWN SUGAR

1 BALL PERFECT PIECRUST DOUGH (SEE PAGE 292)

ALL-PURPOSE FLOUR, FOR DUSTING

DIRECTIONS

1. Preheat the oven to 400°F. Place the mashed sweet potatoes, evaporated milk, eggs, granulated sugar, salt, cinnamon, ginger, and nutmeg in a bowl and stir until combined.

2. Place a cast-iron skillet over medium heat and melt the butter in it. Add the brown sugar and cook, while stirring constantly, until the sugar is dissolved. Remove the pan from heat.

3. Place the piecrust dough on a flour-dusted work surface and roll it out to fit the skillet. Gently place it over the butter-and-brown sugar mixture. Place the skillet in the oven and bake for 15 minutes.

4. Remove the skillet from the oven and briefly let the crust cool. Fill the crust with the sweet potato mixture and use a rubber spatula to evenly distribute. Place the pie in the oven and bake for 15 minutes.

5. Reduce the heat to 325°F and bake until the filling is set and a toothpick inserted in the center comes out clean, about 30 minutes. Remove the skillet from the oven and let cool before serving.

METRIC CONVERSIONS

U.S. Measurement	Approximate Metric Liquid Measurement	Approximate Metric Dry Measurement
1 teaspoon	5 ml	5 g
1 tablespoon or ½ ounce	15 ml	14 g
1 ounce or ⅛ cup	30 ml	29 g
¼ cup or 2 ounces	60 ml	57 g
⅓ cup	80 ml	76 g
½ cup or 4 ounces	120 ml	113 g
⅔ cup	160 ml	151 g
¾ cup or 6 ounces	180 ml	170 g
1 cup or 8 ounces or ½ pint	240 ml	227 g
1½ cups or 12 ounces	350 ml	340 g
2 cups or 1 pint or 16 ounces	475 ml	454 g
3 cups or 1½ pints	700 ml	680 g
4 cups or 2 pints or 1 quart	950 ml	908 g

INDEX

ABOUT CIDER MILL PRESS
BOOK PUBLISHERS

❅ ❅ ❅

Good ideas ripen with time. From seed to harvest,
Cider Mill Press brings fine reading, information,
and entertainment together between the covers of its
creatively crafted books. Our Cider Mill bears fruit twice
a year, publishing a new crop of titles each spring and fall.

CIDER MILL PRESS
BOOK PUBLISHERS
KENNEBUNKPORT, MAINE

"Where Good Books Are Ready for Press"

Visit us online at
cidermillpress.com
or write to us at
PO Box 454
12 Spring St.
Kennebunkport, Maine 04046